Contents

Foreword

Reviewing learners' progress during their journey towards their learning goals is as important as any other part of the learning process, which begins with initial assessment and ends with the assessment of the outcome of that learning.

While previous publications have concentrated on the initial assessment of learners' needs and on the assessment of outcomes in relation to qualifications, this guide sets out to provide you with the knowledge to undertake comprehensive and highly effective progress reviews. The guide has been co-written by Hilary Read, a respected practitioner in the field of work-based learning, and Jane Wells, an occupational psychologist and former lead inspector, now an associate, with the Adult Learning Inspectorate.

To engage learners effectively it is essential to have a way of drawing them into a continuous dialogue with you, from initial assessment right through the process of delivering the high-quality learning they need. This means providing regular and timely meetings with them, where you can discuss and facilitate their progress, intervene where necessary with advice and help with targets, and ultimately assess the outcome of the learning, whether in terms of a qualification or simply – but importantly – in terms of their effectiveness in their job.

The experience of the learner is directly affected by the quality and timing of their progress review. Your interest and encouragement will help support their learning, provide stimulus through agreed targets to continue that learning, and reward them with feedback on their progress. Carrying out regular reviews during learning programmes will ensure that your learners are fully aware of their current position in relation to their learning, and will enable you to help them set objectives for a forthcoming period. Reviews are also a means of measuring whether their objectives have been achieved and of deciding what further action is necessary.

The progress review should be seen as a critical part of every learning programme. It adds the 'cement' to the process and binds all the other aspects together, to ensure that learners achieve their desired outcome at a pace that suits their individual needs.

David Morgan
Director, ENTO

Introduction

Reviewing progress with learners is central to the role of a trainer, and can be one of the most rewarding parts of your job. This guide will not only help you with the practicalities of reviewing progress with your learners, but will also help you understand what reviewing is for, and develop your reviewing skills to ensure that learners achieve their learning targets.

The guide is for everyone responsible for reviewing progress and achievement with learners, including work-based trainers and assessors, and those taking the Certificate in review and assessment of learning (Units L16, G3 and A1).

An effective review process is at the heart of all learning programmes, including:

- work-based learning
- apprenticeships
- learning programmes for getting people back into work or training
- rehabilitation programmes
- vocationally based higher education provision
- 14–16 year-olds involved in vocational learning
- on-job training and development for employees.

The structure of the guide

This guide has the following sections:

Introduction
This explains the principles that underpin effective review.

1 The basics of reviewing
This explains what reviewing is all about and will help you make the most of the guide.

2 Reviewing in action
This section will help you prepare for reviews. It shows you what reviewing is like in practice and how reviewing changes over the course of learners' programmes.

3 The reviewer's toolkit
This section looks at each of the main areas of expertise for the reviewer, which you can refer to according to your needs.

Key principles

Effective reviewing is based on three key principles, which form the central themes of this guide.

1 Learners are at the centre of the review process and are encouraged to take ownership of their own learning and development.

2 Reviews are planned for, structured and purposeful; they are more than just a friendly chat.

3 The organisation values the review process and has procedures and policies in place to support it.

This means:

- encouraging learners to reflect on their learning and progress – what they have learned, how they learned it and ways of improving their performance

- giving learners regular feedback on how well they are doing

- the review process takes account of the learners' development needs, and is not dictated by the assessment system.

- encouraging good relationships and effective partnerships between learners, employers, parents, work-based trainers and assessors.

This means:

- the results of initial assessment are fed directly into the Individual Learning Plan (ILP) and used to inform reviews

- the review process informs the ILP: the ILP may change as a result of review

- long-term goals and short-term targets are negotiated with learners. They change as a result of the review

- the review process informs both learning and assessment. It tells you the point at which summative assessment can usefully begin.

This means:

- reviewing operates within a no-blame culture of learning and building on success within the organisation (as opposed to 'we have to do this every three months because our contract says so')

- reviews are carried out by competent staff who have been trained and equipped with the appropriate skills

- reviewing is seen as a development process in its own right: learners are encouraged to develop new skills by taking part in reviews

- results of review feed into an effective system of recording and tracking progress. Reviews drive the recording system – not the other way round.

About ENTO

ENTO is an independent, self-financing organisation. Since 1988 its purpose has been to develop national vocational standards and qualifications (NVQs) and to provide products and services to support these standards and qualifications.

Our work helps people develop their level of competence and skills, and aims to meet the needs of employees and employers as well as learners. We are also responsible for promoting and monitoring the **matrix** Standard, a quality standard for any organisation that gives information, advice and guidance.

ENTO represents, across all sectors, people whose occupation requires them to deal with people in the workplace. This includes people in the field of information, advice and guidance; learning and development trainers; HR people; recruitment consultants; trade union representatives involved in learning; and health and safety at work practitioners.

Because of this role, the people for whom ENTO standards and qualifications have been developed have a significant influence on the take-up of vocational qualifications throughout the workplace and at all levels. ENTO maintains 9 suites of National Occupational Standards covering 11 occupational areas, 23 NVQs, 4 Apprenticeships and 3 suites of non-qualification-based standards.

The Learning Network

The Learning Network is an online support network run by ENTO for anyone who delivers, assesses or verifies NVQs and SVQs. The network's main aim is to enhance continuous professional development by offering up-to-date information, a forum for discussion and sharing of best practice, and providing the opportunity to influence what is happening in the arena of assessment and verification.

To find out more about the benefits of membership, email: info@ento.co.uk

Alternatively, visit www.thelearningnetworkonline.com or call 02920 462572.

1 The basics of reviewing

Most training providers have review systems in place, which are used as a starting point for monitoring and recording learners' progress. However, making progress doesn't happen by chance. You need to be clear about what reviewing is and what it's for. You also need to think about the climate within which reviewing takes place. For learners to be willing to discuss their progress with you, there needs to be honest, two-way communication based on trust between you and your learner.

This section will help you reflect on what reviewing is for and your approach to reviewing. You will consider:

- *what reviewing is and its main purposes*

- *how it links to learning, assessment, other skills and appraisal*

- *your own review process and how to make the best use of this guide.*

What is reviewing?

Reviewing progress is about helping learners achieve their goals and improve their performance over time. Reviewing is a process whereby you and the learner look back over what has been done, reflect on what has been learned, or why something has not been learned, identify the progress the learner has made, and use the results of this process to inform future action. This in turn leads to further planning and review. Review is often represented as a cycle, like this:

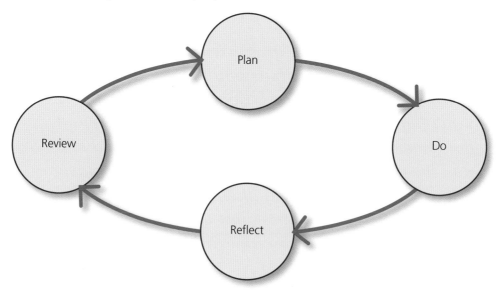

This is a good way of showing what happens during and after a review session. However, it's important not to think of the review process as a closed loop, but as a way to help the learner move forward with their learning. Reviewing is about stepping back and taking a critical look at the broader issues related to skills development and learning, to help you and your learner understand the impact of these on your learner's progress.

What the reviewer does

As the reviewer, you may be involved in some or all of the following activities during a review:

- reviewing progress in learning
- setting goals and targets in relation to what the learner has achieved so far
- planning how these will be met
- giving feedback
- gaining feedback from your learner on their experiences and discussing how they feel
- checking that the programme of learning is still right for the learner (and taking action if necessary)

- dealing with barriers to learning
- agreeing new targets, including timescales for achieving them
- organising opportunities for further learning
- deciding when and how assessment will take place
- assessing progress towards organisational targets
- assessing performance against national standards
- discussing how evidence of performance will be provided
- action planning.

Remember...

Reviewing progress is about much more than the specifics of achieving standards or a qualification. Your main focus should be to encourage learning and development in learners.

Reviewing and the learning process

Over the course of several reviews, the idea is that your learner makes progress towards their goals; the review process shows them how far they've come. The Spiral of Learning[1] below shows how learners make progress over time and how reviewing is linked to the learning process.

The spiral of learning

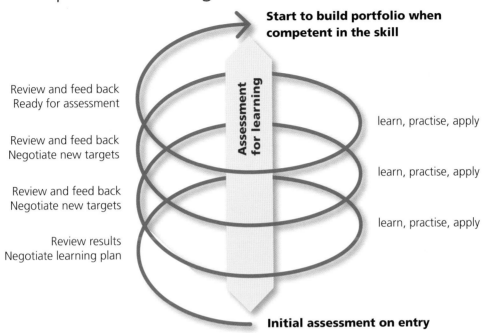

Start to build portfolio when competent in the skill

Review and feed back
Ready for assessment

Review and feed back
Negotiate new targets

Review and feed back
Negotiate new targets

Review results
Negotiate learning plan

Assessment for learning

learn, practise, apply

learn, practise, apply

learn, practise, apply

Initial assessment on entry

At each review, you and your learner review progress towards targets you have agreed at earlier meetings, then negotiate new learning targets or modify existing ones. This leads to further learning, practising and application of these skills. You can also identify the point at which to look for evidence of competence to use for summative assessment purposes – evidence for the learner's portfolio, for example.

You can also use the reviewing process as a vehicle for learners to develop their learning skills. This means making the learning process an *explicit* part of reviewing, and encouraging learners to reflect on their learning and progress.

The learning process means that learners need to:

When reviewing, you need to:

Learn something.	→	Set goals and targets and plan how these will be met.
Practise and apply what they have learned; and continue to learn new things.	→	Reflect and review – gauge what progress has been made. Ask: is the plan working in practice? Modify targets and methods of achieving them, and set action points – things you both need to do next.
Perform competently.	→	Plan for evidence and assessment.

The Kolb Cycle[2]

Understanding the way people learn from concrete experience is relevant to those working with learners on work-based learning programmes, who are in situations where they are learning from direct experience. David Kolb's model of experiential learning is often used in discussions on the theory and practice of adult and lifelong learning. Kolb and his associate Roger Fry created the experiential learning circle (based on the ideas of Kurt Lewin). There are four stages:

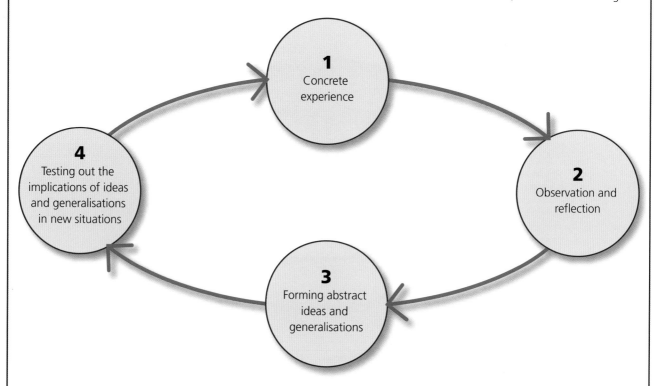

Kolb argued that the learning cycle can begin at any one of the four points, and that it should be approached in the same way as a spiral (like the spiral of learning) so that the process is continuous.

Assessing learning

Assessing learning involves two different types of assessment:

1 Assessment *for* learning[3] (also called formative assessment)

Assessment for learning goes on throughout the learning process and is the main focus of the progress review. This is where you look at the progress the learner has made in their learning – checking what they've learned and if they've understood, how they've learned and whether or not the ways of learning you've agreed are working in practice. Assessing for learning is about you and your learner deciding what's working and what isn't, and using this to inform your next steps.

2 Assessment *of* learning (also called summative assessment)

This involves assessing evidence of the learner's performance against predetermined standards or criteria. The process 'sums up' where the learner is at a given point, and can involve methods like practical testing or written exams. Planning for assessment of learning is different from assessing for learning, and you don't usually carry out assessment *of* learning until assessment *for* learning has taken place. Your main focus during progress reviews will be about assessment for learning.

---

2 Experience Based Learning Systems, Inc. Reproduced with permission.

3 This term was first used by the Assessment Reform Group, *Assessment for Learning: Beyond the Black Box* (Cambridge: School of Education, Cambridge University, 1999).

'I see many progress reviews where the main activity is looking at progress towards the qualification and planning for summative assessment. Learners who only take part in this sort of review talk in terms of their qualification – not their learning or progress. Assessors can and do carry out progress reviews in relation to the qualification, but reviewing progress in learning has an entirely different focus.'
Inspector

The benefits of assessment for learning

Research has shown that learners benefit from assessment *for* learning in the following ways:

- they become more confident learners because they can see themselves succeeding

- they are more likely to want to continue learning – an important consideration for disaffected learners who may have failed in the past

- achievement rates improve

- over time, learners gradually start to take control of their own learning – the basis of lifelong learning.

Trainers also benefit because:

- learners are more motivated to learn

- results of formative assessment can be used to inform the quality of training, which can then be tailored to meet learners' needs.

Links to other skills and qualifications

You need to think of reviewing as a partnership between you and the learner – one where you encourage your learner to think critically about the progress they have made and ultimately to take charge of their own learning and development. For this, learners need to 'see' what they are learning and be involved in decisions about what they learn and how to tackle learning. This also means making process skills such as learning to learn and reflection an explicit part of the review process.

What training providers say

'Reviewing with learners at the start of their programmes helps to set the scene when building a partnership. Reviews then become an opportunity to discuss learning involving the learner rather than a judgement – something that's done to them.'
Reviewer

'As a training provider, reviews provide us with a regular opportunity to check on how we are doing in the eyes of our customers – the learners'.
Trainer

'Reviews raise our game. They empower learners to develop and voice their preferences. Learners seek out effective teaching and learning and ask what they will be able to do as the result of a training session.'
Trainer

'As an employer, reviews help us link the skills and knowledge being developed to the work context. This gives a purpose to learning and helps staff to measure its effectiveness through the development of competencies at work.'
Training manager

'To me, reviewing learners' progress isn't just about planning and progress (tasks to do and ones they've achieved). It's also enabling learners to be more aware of their approaches to learning – the ways they learn best, and why. This is the most important part of reviewing, in my opinion'
Trainer

Spending time developing these skills with learners at the beginning of their programmes pays dividends in the longer term, as they learn how to reflect and begin to take an active part in improving their performance. Using the review process for this means you can actively encourage learners to develop these and other skills, including:

- **learning skills**, such as learning to learn and choosing and using different ways of learning

- **lifelong learning**, the ability to identify your own learning needs and choose appropriate methods of learning throughout your working and personal life

- **the wider key skills**, which are:
  - improving own learning and performance
  - working with others
  - problem solving.

It's worth noting that the key skill of improving own learning and performance is the review process when carried out effectively with learners. Again, you need to make the skills of improving learning and performance explicit and actively develop them if you want learners to achieve them – they don't learn them automatically simply by participating in the review process.

- **employability skills:** these are skills that employers value and concern a person's ability to gain and hold down a job, and include:
  - basic literacy, numeracy and language skills
  - learning to learn and career management skills
  - occupational skills
  - developing positive attitudes to work
  - teamwork skills.

Reviewing and appraisal

Many organisations carry out regular performance appraisals with staff as a matter of course. The appraisal process is similar to the review process except that, whereas reviewing takes place in the learning context, appraisals take place within the organisational context.

Typically, employees have their first appraisal three months after joining a company, followed by annual appraisals. Before each appraisal, the individual reviews their own performance and records their opinions. The person carrying out the appraisal also reviews the employee's performance and records it on a standard form. Similarities and differences of opinion then form the basis of discussion during the appraisal.

Further differences between reviewing and appraisal could be that:

- appraisals assume that the person being appraised is already working to a predetermined standard

- the appraisee may not be seen as a learner or may not be treated as a partner during the appraisal

(the person carrying out the appraisal may be in a position of authority, such as a manager)

- the individual's targets may be linked to organisational targets or job descriptions rather than personal learning goals

- there may be less scope for negotiation

- the person carrying out the appraisal acts on behalf of the organisation rather than the appraisee

- achievement of targets may be directly linked to rewards (promotion or pay increases) or disciplinary procedures if performance falls below expectations.

Effective organisations do take account of individual needs and encourage employees to pursue their goals, since this has a positive effect on motivation, morale and productivity. Organisations do, of course, employ learners such as apprentices on work-based learning programmes with organisational performance and productivity in mind. However, the learner needs to undergo a programme of learning and development before he or she can contribute to an organisation meaningfully.

Self-check: audit your review process

Is your reviewing process working? What about your own (or your staff's) knowledge and skills in reviewing? Answer the following questions honestly.

Question	Yes	No	Not sure
1 Do you know what you want your review process to do?	☐	☐	☐
2 Do reviews tell you what you need to know about learners' progress?	☐	☐	☐
3 Do learners play an active part in reviews?	☐	☐	☐
4 Does everybody know what they are reviewing and why?	☐	☐	☐
5 Do you revisit previous reviews (and make sure you pick up where you left off last time) to ensure progression?	☐	☐	☐
6 Are the results of reviews acted upon?	☐	☐	☐
7 Are reviews planned and structured (or do they just 'happen')?	☐	☐	☐
8 Do you know how to set targets with learners?	☐	☐	☐
9 Do you give learners feedback on how well they are doing?	☐	☐	☐
10 Do you ask learners to reflect on their progress?	☐	☐	☐
11 Do you set action points as a result of reviews?	☐	☐	☐
12 Does your recording system tell you where all your learners are in relation to their targets?	☐	☐	☐
13 Do you have recording tools that encourage learners to reflect?	☐	☐	☐
14 Can you tell if your review process is working? (In other words, do you quality assure against a clear set of criteria?)	☐	☐	☐
15 Do you seek the views of learners and other key players (like employers) on the effectiveness of your reviews?	☐	☐	☐

You are aiming to answer yes in all cases. Where you have answered no or not sure, turn to the relevant section of the guide, as follows:

Number	Section
1, 5, 6	Reviewing in action, page 19
2	Reviewing in action: Planning review sessions, page 20
	The reviewer's toolkit: Quality assurance, page 77
3, 10, 13	The reviewer's toolkit: Encouraging reflection, page 54
4, 7	Reviewing in action: Planning review sessions, page 20
8	The reviewer's toolkit: Setting targets, page 44
9	The reviewer's toolkit: Giving feedback, page 60
11	The reviewer's toolkit: Action planning, page 65
12	The reviewer's toolkit: Recording progress, page 68
14, 15	The reviewer's toolkit: Quality assurance, page 77

What the standards say

If you plan to use this guide to develop and improve your skills in reviewing and are working towards the Learning and Development units, you may find the following links helpful:

Unit L16 Monitor and review progress with learners

Performance criteria	Turn to the section entitled...
a Base your reviews of progress on the views of learners and your assessment of their progress to date	Reviewing in action
c Encourage learners to express their views on their own progress	The reviewer's toolkit: Encouraging reflection
b Check that the information you use in the review with learners is accurate and unbiased	Reviewing in action: Planning review sessions
d Match information to learning objectives to see what learners have achieved	Reviewing in action
e Give learners positive feedback	The reviewer's toolkit: Giving feedback
f Identify new learning needs and objectives	The reviewer's toolkit: Setting targets
g Identify and agree any changes to the learning programme as a result of the review	Reviewing in action
h Record, pass on and use the results of the review	The reviewer's toolkit: Recording progress

Knowledge: How to...	
1 Involve learners in the review and assessment processes	The reviewer's toolkit: Encouraging reflection
2 Encourage individuals and groups to take part in the review process	Reviewing in action: Planning review sessions
3 Set and renegotiate learning objectives	The reviewer's toolkit: Setting targets
4 Match the results of reviews to the changes the learning programmes require	The reviewer's toolkit: Quality assurance
5 Collect and analyse information for review and assessment purposes	Reviewing in action: Planning review sessions The reviewer's toolkit: Quality assurance
6 Identify and use appropriate sources of reliable and valid information	Reviewing in action
7 Prioritise and summarise information correctly	Reviewing in action
8 Record and store information for review and assessment purposes	The reviewer's toolkit: Recording progress
9 Use information technology to keep records	The reviewer's toolkit: Recording progress

10	Put learners at their ease	The reviewer's toolkit: Recording progress
11	Give learners constructive feedback	The reviewer's toolkit: Recording progress
12	Put information in order	The reviewer's toolkit: Giving feedback The reviewer's toolkit: Encouraging reflection
13	Apply interview and discussion techniques	The reviewer's toolkit: Giving feedback The reviewer's toolkit: Encouraging reflection
14	Ensure that everyone acts in line with health, safety and environmental protection legislation and best practice	Reviewing in action The reviewer's toolkit: Recording progress
15	Identify and apply relevant legislation to individuals' rights	The reviewer's toolkit: Giving feedback

Reflecting on your own practice

Use the table below to jot down:

- any personal development needs you may have
- how you plan to use the guide to help you as a reviewer.

Use your answers to the activity on page 13 to assist you with this.

Links to Unit G3, Evaluate and develop your own practice

G3.1 Evaluate your own practice
I need to develop in these areas…

G3.2 Identify your self-development needs
I plan to use the guide as follows…

2 Reviewing in action

Skilled reviewers know how to plan and prepare for reviewing so that both the learners and their organisation make the most of the time and resources available. This part of the guide takes you through the reviewing process so that you'll know what to concentrate on and when. The process covers:

- ***planning review sessions.** This involves considering the timing and frequency of reviews according to the support needs of the individual learner. This section looks at different types of review and what reviews broadly need to cover, and gives ideas for how to structure a session.*

- ***facilitating progress.** This tells you about the early stages of the review process, including finding out about the learner through the ILP and initial assessment, and using this knowledge to plan for learning and help your learner set initial targets.*

- ***reviewing targets and planning for assessment.** Later on in the process you'll be looking for opportunities for learners to put their newly acquired knowledge and skills into practice as well as continuing to plan for learning to take place. You'll also need to take account of summative assessment once the learner starts to perform to the required standard.*

Planning review sessions

Preparing for reviews with learners involves making decisions about how often to review and the type of reviews to use. The way you review will change over time, depending on the stage the learner has reached in their programme and their individual learning needs and circumstances. Responding to learners' development needs also affects the target-setting process and how you deal with issues that arise.

Reviews should vary in their frequency and depth. It's important to plan for this, or the review process can become a mechanical one for you ('We do this every three months.') or boring for the learner ('Why are we doing this? I don't think I've done much, really.'). When planning, you need to take account of:

- the support needs of your learners and the characteristics of the learning programme

- the different types of review, such as face-to-face or group reviews.

Considering support needs

New learners on long learning programmes need support and a progress review within four to six weeks of starting. Learners may be new to the world of work, and struggle with the transition from school, where they were equals, into work where relationships are more complex. They may feel nervous about how to make friends, unclear about their job role and confused about how the learning programme works.

Learners with little confidence might need a high degree of support, particularly in the beginning, and you'll find that some learners always need more support than others. If you are not able to provide this, then you should enlist the help of a workplace 'buddy' or mentor.

Established, confident learners may need little support once they are clear about what they are doing, and they can quickly become self-directed learners. These learners are going to be pushing for assessment and always wanting to 'get on with it'. Reviews with this group are likely to be swift and businesslike, and the learner may even perceive the review process as unnecessary, but you will still need to encourage them to develop the skills of self-reflection and evaluation.

Learners in danger of leaving and those with problems may need high-level monitoring and support. You may need to review their progress frequently, perhaps as often as every four weeks in the case of an apprenticeship. You may want to give telephone or email support in between as well. You will often find that learners who need high-level monitoring at first simply need a period of 'intensive care' over a difficult time and will eventually need less support. Some may leave, but if they have had a chance to explore the issues with your support, they may well come back into learning later.

Timing reviews

Just as learning programmes vary in length, so will the frequency of your reviews. Some programmes may last only one day, while others can go on indefinitely – for example, those for people with disabilities wishing to develop their skills in the workplace. The following chart gives suggestions for how often to review, based on the programme and the kinds of support learners may need.

Ideally, you should plan the timing of reviews according to the needs of the learner (using the guidelines in the table as the minimum). The 'What to look for and why' column contains specific suggestions for the type of programme, but don't base your review purely on these.

Programme type	Example	When to review	What to look for and why
Short courses	Six one-hour sessions using an e-learning package	Approximately halfway through. It is useful to take time away from the computer at this point, to look at what has been learned, any problems and difficulties and what has worked well.	Ensure that the programme suits the learner and that they are motivated to continue.
School or unemployment to work programmes	Entry to employment (E2e)	As frequently as possible (at least every four weeks), and preferably weekly, focusing on a different aspect of the programme each time.	Learners on these programmes often engage in a wide range of learning activities to develop their literacy, numeracy, vocational and interpersonal skills. They will have many targets, and the complexity of their programme may mean that they forget their targets or achievements if the gap between reviews is too long. Concentrate on one aspect of their learning at a time. For the programme to be really motivating and tailored to the individual, be prepared for it to change significantly at each review.
Vocational training (1)	Apprenticeships	At least three-monthly (ideally, planned around the development needs of the apprentice).	Here your main task is to ensure that all those with a role to play – employers, college tutors or company trainers – tell you about previous goals and targets so that you can agree any changes to the programme as the learner progresses.
Vocational training (2)	Workstep	At least six-monthly. You need to be flexible around the learner's individual needs and circumstances. Learners will need more frequent reviews if they are hoping to move into open employment shortly, or if they are receiving help in learning to do a new job.	Here you need to concentrate on reviewing employability as well as personal skills and abilities. You may also need to consider literacy, numeracy and ICT skills. Employees in declining health may need support to enable them to maintain their existing employment, and here you'll need to consider frequent reviews of a range of needs .

Types of review session

All reviews are about:

- identifying needs and planning learning
- building relationships and encouraging learners
- getting learners used to the review process.

This means:

- arranging learning and development activities, including catering for any special needs the learner may have
- identifying early successes and giving feedback on these
- encouraging your learner to begin to reflect on their learning
- checking against the ILP to ensure that the overall goals are the right ones and to ensure that the targets set at the outset are realistic and achievable
- setting further learning targets to enable learners to acquire the necessary knowledge, skills and attitudes to achieve their goals.

For each review session to be effective – enabling learners to understand what they have achieved, what they need to achieve and identifying problems and barriers along the way – it will take time. For a three-year learning programme, you are likely to need two hours per session. Many reviews may have to take place in less than ideal circumstances such as a crowded staff room or in the learner's lunch break, without the support of their employer.

Self-check: looking at the options

Whatever the circumstances in which you carry out reviews, take a critical look at the opportunities and constraints, and ask yourself:

	Yes	No
Do reviews take place entirely on a face-to-face basis?	☐	☐
Is there a place for different ways of reviewing?	☐	☐
Can I use e-technology instead of face-to-face contact?	☐	☐
Could other key people (like the employer or college tutor) be more fully involved?	☐	☐

If you've answered yes to any of these, you may want to consider using a variety of types of review with each learner.

The main types of review are one-to-one sessions face to face, one-to-one sessions via e-technology, and group sessions.

One-to-one, face-to-face reviews

This is the most common type of review and is probably the one people feel most comfortable with. However, while reviewers and learners enjoy sitting down and talking over how things are going, this isn't always the best strategy, either for the learner or for the reviewer's organisation. Well-managed, face-to-face reviews can be highly productive, but they depend on careful planning and preparation in order to be effective, so that learners move on and make continuous progress.

One-to-one, face-to-face reviews have certain advantages and disadvantages, as follows:

Advantages

You develop ongoing, consistent rapport with your learners, allowing them to feel comfortable about discussing issues as they arise.

The most effective way of meeting a learner's individual needs through detailed target setting.

Gives the opportunity to develop good rapport with employers and workplace supervisors. Employers are actively encouraged to be involved in the learner's progress.

Disadvantages

It can be expensive, especially if learners are scattered across a wide geographical area and staff have to spend hours travelling. Even if your learners are in a smaller area, going to them can prove inefficient time-wise.

You need enough skilled reviewers in the right place at the right time to meet the needs of individual learners.

Learners may not get on with the person responsible for carrying out their review and may be reluctant to contribute fully.

Structuring a one-to-one review session

The way you structure your review session with learners will have an impact on their ability and motivation to achieve the targets you've agreed. They should leave the session with a clear understanding of what they need to do next. To help with this it's useful to divide the session into three distinct parts, each with its own activities.

The beginning

- Re-establish rapport
- Restate what was agreed at the last review
- Agree what you both want out of this review.

The middle

- Encourage the learner to reflect on their progress
- Check general aspects of the learner's well-being
- Refer back to the ILP
- Thoroughly review progress, including achievements and areas of difficulty and give feedback on performance
- Consider options and decide next steps
- Agree SMART targets
- Identify action points
- Check understanding
- Seek real agreement by observing the learner's body language and checking that yes *means* yes.

The end

- Fill in any documentation by helping learners to put things into their own words
- Recap on what has been said and decided. If *you* can't sum it up clearly, the chances are that the learner is confused as well
- Check that the learner *really* understands by asking questions
- End with a positive motivational statement like: 'I think you've got plans for a great project there – I'm really looking forward to seeing the results next time.'

One-to-one reviews via e-technology

Carrying out reviews entirely by e-technology is not recommended, for the reasons given below, but can prove a useful supplementary method and is a good way of keeping learners engaged and motivated. You can structure the session in a broadly similar way to a face-to-face session.

Advantages

For learners who need frequent checking because of particular problems, e-technology enables you to review progress between face-to-face reviews.

Time and cost efficient.

Employers can see a copy, by prior agreement of course, and may add their comments at a time convenient to them. This overcomes the problem of employers being too busy to be involved in the review.

Disadvantages

You can't pick up on body language or verbal clues because you can't see the learner. All you have to go on is the text.

Some learners may be reluctant to disclose issues using a permanent medium ('writing it down' via an email).

It's difficult to include anyone else fully in the process.

There is growing evidence that using information technology such as email is as important to engaging with learners as finding their preferred way of learning. Recording evidence and communicating with tutors electronically are well-established methodologies that encourage learners actively to engage more frequently and to provide a varied range of evidence.

'I access my e-portfolios in the wee small hours of the morning! I'm a night owl and it's peaceful then.' Assessor

'I work in the security industry – a lot of night work. I find email and telephone are the best ways of keeping in touch with my tutor. I prefer to talk as well as email.' Learner

Group reviews

If your learners have a time when they meet up with their peers, you can take advantage of the opportunity to review progress. It works like this:

- Learners take time out from their work or training to review their own progress (for example, a two-hourly slot every three months from a total of 12 weekly sessions).

- Learners know the format of the session and come prepared.

- They are sent a checklist or review sheet in advance (one that follows their face-to-face format or one that they are familiar with).

- They know what they are going to be reflecting and working on during the review session.

Here's an example of a half-day group session plan to give you some ideas. You don't have to include everything in one session: for example, the equality and diversity session could take place on another day. You might also want to invite the learners' tutors or employers to watch the presentations. Keep group sessions general; it's best to deal with personal or individual issues on a one-to-one basis.

Group session plan

Course title: *Group progress reviews*   **Date:** Thursday 16 June   **Venue:** Training centre

Time	Topic	Method/ resources	Tutor notes
10 mins	*Introduction and session objectives*	Flipchart or PowerPoint	Explain what the session's about and what will be happening.
30 mins	*What have you achieved?*	Log books, ILPs, learning logs, progress reports from employers and/or tutors	In groups of three, ask each person to spend five minutes reviewing their progress against their own SMART targets. Each person then to list what they were pleased about and share this with the other two. Tutor to circulate and offer help as necessary.
30 mins	*Exploring problems and difficulties*	As above	In their small groups, ask each person to identify areas where they have not achieved targets and to explain why not. Ask the group to put forward suggestions for solving any problems. Make sure everyone gets a turn.
30 mins	*Setting SMART targets*	Flip chart or OHTs and coloured pens or laptops and data projector	Spend five to ten minutes reminding learners how to set a target if necessary. In pairs, ask learners to help each other set SMART targets for next time. Set a maximum of two or three targets per person. Circulate and make sure everyone sets targets.
15 mins	*Break*		
45 mins	*Presentations*	As above	Ask each group to present their progress reports to the whole group.
60 mins	***Equality and diversity:*** *1 Equal opportunities*	Flipchart	Take a few minutes to explain the principles behind EO and H&SAW legislation and why it's important if you think learners need reminding. List the main areas so that learners have suggested topics in front of them. In small groups, ask learners to focus on one aspect (for example: harassment or assessing risks). Ask them to discuss the issues to do with the way in which people are treated and how they treat others in the workplace and to record any general issues.
	1 Health and safety		Follow the same process for health and safety. Allow 20 minutes for groups to share issues and discuss them with the whole group.
30 mins	*Quantifying progress*		Ask learners to assess 'how much' they've achieved over the last review period and to express this as a percentage of their 'whole'. Give prizes to those who've come a long way. Ask them for proof. (In other words, learners need to justify their percentage and back it up with hard evidence.) Get the group to vote for the best effort or for the person they think has succeeded or overcome a problem in the most original way.

You will need to have already run a session on target-setting for this to work.

Once learners become familiar with this process, they can be as imaginative as they like. You may want to use other materials and/or media for this.

Keep a note of things to follow up with learners individually, and pass this information on if necessary.

Keep this light-hearted – it's a fun activity.

This format often works because some learners perform better when:

- there is an element of competition
- they are being watched
- they get support from peers
- they perceive pressure from peers
- authority figures are not directly in control.

Advantages	Disadvantages
Time and cost efficient.	Learners who are not making good progress may skip the session. You must keep a close eye on this and arrange to see any absentees on their own.
Peer pressure is often more effective than pressure from reviewers/authority figures.	It is harder to establish a rapport with employers and gain their full involvement.
Learners can see what others are achieving and react positively if they think that they will be left behind.	Learners may not be willing to share some issues of equality of opportunity in this setting. You'll need to talk to each learner individually to find out whether they have any significant concerns.
Learners see and learn how others approach learning goals, and get constructive feedback from their peers (provided the session is well facilitated).	Needs commitment and preparation from learners to work well. (Once established, though, the process develops a momentum of its own.)
A useful way for learners to develop the wider key skills of improving own learning and performance, working with others and problem solving.	Needs careful facilitating by a skilled tutor.

'Group and peer reviews are a wonderful way of familiarising learners with the process of reflecting on their own progress. You've got the experience and expertise of the whole group at your disposal and you use this to help individuals see alternatives and solve problems.'

Trainer

Facilitating progress

During the first part of learners' programmes your role is to identify needs and plan for learning to take place, and to ensure that your learners make progress in their learning. Even in the early stages learners will want you to give them concrete information about how well they are doing, but you may not know much about them. Before you start reviewing you'll need to gather information from the following sources:

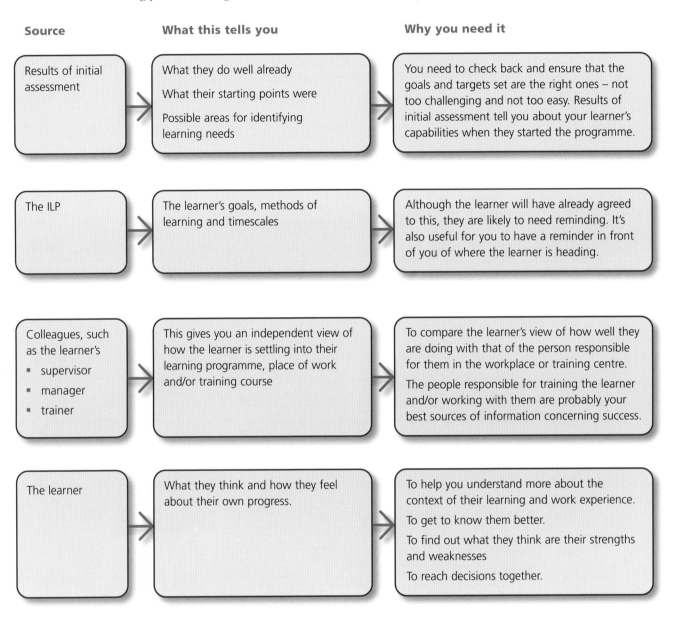

Source	What this tells you	Why you need it
Results of initial assessment	What they do well already What their starting points were Possible areas for identifying learning needs	You need to check back and ensure that the goals and targets set are the right ones – not too challenging and not too easy. Results of initial assessment tell you about your learner's capabilities when they started the programme.
The ILP	The learner's goals, methods of learning and timescales	Although the learner will have already agreed to this, they are likely to need reminding. It's also useful for you to have a reminder in front of you of where the learner is heading.
Colleagues, such as the learner's • supervisor • manager • trainer	This gives you an independent view of how the learner is settling into their learning programme, place of work and/or training course	To compare the learner's view of how well they are doing with that of the person responsible for them in the workplace or training centre. The people responsible for training the learner and/or working with them are probably your best sources of information concerning success.
The learner	What they think and how they feel about their own progress.	To help you understand more about the context of their learning and work experience. To get to know them better. To find out what they think are their strengths and weaknesses To reach decisions together.

Effective reviews during these early stages are based on the results of initial assessment and an individual learning plan (ILP) agreed with the individual that meets their needs. The review process means giving learners enough information to enable them to take part and make informed decisions. Your main focus at this stage should be on planning for learning in areas where initial assessment has identified a need.

In the early stages of review, check with the learner that the learning programme you have agreed, the timescales and the methods of learning are working in practice. If they aren't, you'll need to do something about it. It's important to anticipate changes and make adjustments in the early stages (rather than leaving it until the end of their programme).

Using the ILP and initial assessment

Since early reviews are linked to the results of initial assessment and the ILP, information from both of these will inform the decisions you make during the sessions. The results of initial assessment tell you about your learners' aspirations, attainments and potential as well as highlighting areas where they may need extra help. Effective initial assessment forms the basis of a realistic ILP, which lists overall goals and targets based on each learner's particular needs and also details their route to achieving them.

Here are the main areas included on an ILP:

- Goals and targets

- Learning activities (planning how the goals and targets will be met)

- Arrangements for assessment and review

- Who's involved

- Resources needed

- Dates and timescales for achievement.

Remember...

1 The ILP is your overall plan. You will need this at each review to check progress overall. If you find that your learner is not progressing, you may need to change the ILP.

2 Initial assessment isn't a one-off event. During the early stages of learners' programmes you may be assessing their capabilities on the job or their occupational suitability, and giving feedback over the course of several reviews.

3 You may also need to refer to the results of initial assessment during early reviews, to help you gauge how well your learner is doing.

'Our apprentices do a stint in each area of the factory, then they specialise after the first year. We do this through a process of continual assessment and negotiation with the individual concerned. It's obvious to them and to us what they're good at by this time.'

Training manager, engineering

Self-check: the ILP and the review process

Does your initial assessment system give you all the information you need as the reviewer? Do you use the ILP? Answer the following questions to see if you are maintaining adequate links. You are aiming to answer yes in each case.

Are the results of initial assessment...	Yes	No
Passed on to you, the reviewer?	☐	☐
Acted upon?	☐	☐
Fed back to the learner concerned?	☐	☐
Used as the basis for each learner's ILP?	☐	☐
Used to inform the goal and target-setting process in the early stages?	☐	☐
Do you ...		
Refer to the ILP during reviews?	☐	☐
Modify it if necessary?	☐	☐
Take action if the ILP isn't working in practice?	☐	☐

Where you have answered no, you will need to take action. For further help on planning ILPs with learners and initial assessment, consult the ENTO guide *Excellence in initial assessment*.

Here are extracts from an ILP along with the results of an early review.

TARDIS ELECTRICAL UK LTD
Individual Learning Plan

Here is a brief summary of the results of Joe's initial assessment

Name: Joe Lewis

Manager: Ed Bates

Department: Warehouse

Learning Mentor: Grace Sinclair

INITIAL ASSESSMENT

Method	What was assessed?	Outcomes/recommendations
1 Interview	Career goals	Joe would like to become an electrical engineer in the company where his father works.
2 Reference from employer/workplace experience	Occupational suitability	He has worked part-time in the company for the past 2 years and they have offered to employ him.
3 GCSE results	Essential and Key skills	Joe has Maths GCSE Grade B, English Grade C and ICT Grade D. He would like to improve his ICT skills as he is not confident in this area and needs to learn how to use company software.
4 Self-assessment and discussion	Preferred ways of learning	Joe likes to learn by doing and enjoys practical tasks. He is happy to learn on his own. He dislikes studying and reading. Recommend self-study package and one-to-one support for ICT.

GOALS

1 To learn how to use the Internet by the last Thursday in October 2005.

2 To achieve the ICT Key skill Level 2 by June 2006.

These form part of Joe's ILP

LEARNING TARGETS

1 To learn how to input and print off a job sheet accurately and to the manager's satisfaction by 30 June 2005.

2 To learn to use a search engine to identify three electrical suppliers approved by the manager by 30 June 2005.

3 To learn how to enter numerical data and use the SUM formula accurately on a spreadsheet package by 30 June 2005.

SUMMARY OF INITIAL REVIEW

Learner's comments

I want to learn how to use a computer as I have to input my job sheets using the company software. I wasn't good at this at school. I hated being in a large group because I felt stupid asking for help. I'm enjoying my job and really want to get started on my NVQ units.

I know I have to settle into my job and training first. I'm going to keep a learning log and a work file of all the things I do in the first three months.

Reviewer's comments

In view of Joe's past experiences with ICT and the way he likes to learn, I've spoken to Andy Brooks (the IT tutor) and will arrange for Joe to attend our Thursday drop-in session where he will receive one-to-one help. We've discussed the major tasks Joe does at work. At the moment he's learning how to use the tools of the trade and basic health and safety and housekeeping routines. Joe starts a rewiring project at work next week. We've provisionally picked two optional and two core units of his NVQ but I've asked him to check these with Ed in a week or two. I've given Andy a work-in-progress file for his job sheets and ICT work. He's also agreed to keep a learning log.

Note how the reviewer liaised with the IT tutor in this case. If you are not a specialist in the area where your learner has a need, ask the appropriate person for help with setting specific targets.

LEARNING ARRANGEMENTS

Learning/ course title	Where will it take place?	Who will monitor progress?	Attendance arrangements
ICT Level 2	IT Centre	Andy and Grace	Thursday afternoons

Action points	Who	By when	
Book ICT sessions	Grace	Next Friday	
Arrange to practise filling in a job sheet under supervision	Joe to talk to Ed	Tomorrow	
Ring Joe to check that the NVQ units we've chosen are the right ones	Grace	20 April	

You need to revisit targets, learning arrangements and action planning, and set new review dates each time you review.

REVIEW ARRANGEMENTS

3-monthly review date	Person responsible	Location
30/06/05	Grace	Training department

It's important to include the frequency of reviews here. Learning targets have been planned around the next review date.

Signed (Employee):	Signed (Mentor):	Date:
Joe Lewis	Grace Sinclair	3 April 2005

Setting initial targets

Principles to bear in mind when target setting at this stage are:

- Focus on one or two learning needs at a time and link these to the learner's NVQ or technical certificate.

- If you are dealing with work-based learners, identify one or two of their main job tasks and use these as the basis for setting learning targets. If they are working towards an NVQ, link these to the optional and core units so that learners understand the relevance of what they will be learning.

- If you identify a learning need, think in terms of two or three linked learning targets (as in the example on the previous two pages), so the learner knows exactly what they're aiming for.

- Set small, achievable targets in the early stages. If learners aren't making much progress, the targets may be too broad for them to be able to see that they're achieving.

'We involve our assessor in planning for assessment from the start. She helps identify one or two appropriate units to focus on – usually ones that involve tasks the learner does as part of their routine work or where they are already pretty confident. We find that this gives them concrete success and builds motivation.'

Training manager

You need to get the balance right. Introduce the learner to summative assessment when you can show that learning has taken place first, or when the learner already has evidence that they are performing to standard. In the first part of learners' programmes, though, your main focus is on planning and reviewing learning.

For more on how to set effective learning targets, see the section on target setting on page 42.

Discussing policies and procedures

In addition to discussing the goals agreed in their ILPs, during the early stages you should remind learners about your policies and procedures and when they apply.

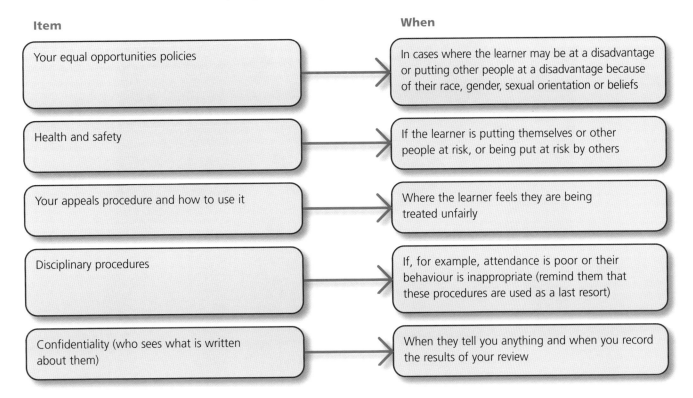

Item | **When**

Item	When
Your equal opportunities policies	In cases where the learner may be at a disadvantage or putting other people at a disadvantage because of their race, gender, sexual orientation or beliefs
Health and safety	If the learner is putting themselves or other people at risk, or being put at risk by others
Your appeals procedure and how to use it	Where the learner feels they are being treated unfairly
Disciplinary procedures	If, for example, attendance is poor or their behaviour is inappropriate (remind them that these procedures are used as a last resort)
Confidentiality (who sees what is written about them)	When they tell you anything and when you record the results of your review

Here are some examples of the kinds of questions that you might want to ask the learner during a review session. This is not an exhaustive list and you may need to construct prompt sheets for use across your organisation. (This will also help with your quality assurance.)

Equal opportunities

- How do you get on with your colleagues, supervisors and/or managers? Do you like them? (If not, explore why not; you may find that the learner is being bullied.)
- Do you like the tasks you are given? Are your colleagues given similar unpleasant/boring tasks to do? (If not, explore why not.)
- Has anyone been promoted since the last time we met? Did everyone have the opportunity to apply for promotion?
- Who has been on a training course? Did you want to go? Why didn't you get the opportunity?
- When did you last have a pay rise/bonus? Is that the same as everyone else?

Health and safety

- Have you had any cuts or bruises at work?
- Have you slipped on anything or tripped over anything?
- Has anyone hurt themselves since we last met? What happened?
- Have there been any 'near misses'? Were they reported? Did any changes occur as a result?
- Do you find any of the equipment hard to use or tasks hard or awkward to do?
- If 'yes', have you received training? Or is the job too difficult for your level of experience?

In summary

When you review during the early stages of learners' programmes, it is important to show them that they are making progress – no matter how small or insignificant it may seem – as this will motivate them to continue. This means:

- **being prepared** – make sure you've collected the information you need on the learner's progress before the review takes place. Importantly, during the early stages you should be referring to results of initial assessment and the ILP.

- **focusing on reviewing progress – helping the learner see how far they've come.** Learners need time to learn things during the early stages of their programmes.

*'I joined a running club but as a relatively unfit female
I was always the slowest in the group. However, one day two
new women joined and I was asked to coach them. I didn't
realise until then how much I had improved since I'd started
until I had someone less experienced to compare my
performance with!'*

Trainer

Reviewing targets and planning for assessment

As well as continuing to acquire new skills and knowledge, in the medium term learners need the opportunity to practise and apply what they have learnt so that they become competent at what they are doing. In addition, you will be planning for assessment as learners begin to perform to the required standards.

Questions to ask the learner at this stage include:

- What new tasks have you tried since last time?

- What can you do now that you couldn't do last time?

- What have you found difficult? Challenging? Exciting? Interesting?

Use questions like these to identify and explore problems such as incompatibility of learning styles, wrong occupational choice, or intention to leave. Don't avoid these issues. Unhappy learners usually welcome the opportunity to talk and you will often be in a position to do something about their problem.

Mid-term reviews

In the medium term you will continue to check that targets are being achieved, in particular:

- modifying existing targets and adding more challenging ones

- taking action in areas where the learner is not making adequate progress or needs help

- finding new and varied opportunities for the learner to practise and apply what they are learning

- recognising when learners are performing to agreed standards and planning for summative assessment (you may need to involve the assessor at this point)

- helping learners to gather evidence of their performance.

Modifying targets

As learners make progress, so their targets will change. As they become more confident learners, you will be able to agree more challenging targets with them. 'Challenging' could mean:

- tackling an area of learning the learner finds difficult

- trying out a new way of learning

- experimenting and being creative

- allowing the learner to be at the centre of the target-setting process and take the lead

- analysing mistakes or 'failures' and turning these into opportunities for learning

- performing the same task, but gradually withdrawing supervision and support

- taking a more holistic approach to learning by aiming for several targets at once or covering more than one topic

- practising the same task or applying the same knowledge under different circumstances or conditions.

Ideally, you should be doing all these things with learners so that they increase in confidence and become competent learners as well as ensuring they meet all the requirements of the standards. (For more help with target setting, see page 42.)

Barriers to progress

You will come across barriers to learners making progress, and you need to recognise them and deal with them. Two common ones are low self-esteem and learners saying yes when they mean no.

Low self-esteem

If feedback is to be useful then the learner needs to hear it, take it in and act on it. One important barrier to learners accepting feedback is low self-esteem. Learners with low self-esteem need a lot of encouragement and positive comments to believe in their own competence and achievement. You can recognise them because they are likely to dismiss the positive and only hear the negative. They do this to seek confirmation of their perception of themselves and feel that tutors and assessors are being positive just to be nice.

The intention behind your feedback may also be significant. If you use feedback to 'pass judgement' on the learner's performance, this is different from giving feedback to enable them to see for themselves how well they are doing. Here, you're about facilitating development and the learner is more likely to respond positively.

When learners say yes...

At the end of a review, when you have summarised the learner's achievements and what they need to do for the next period, inevitably you will ask the learner to sign something to say that they have agreed. You might say, 'So you're clear about what you need to do before I see you again?' and the learner might say 'yes', but mean 'no'. There are several possible reasons for this, set out below with suggested responses.

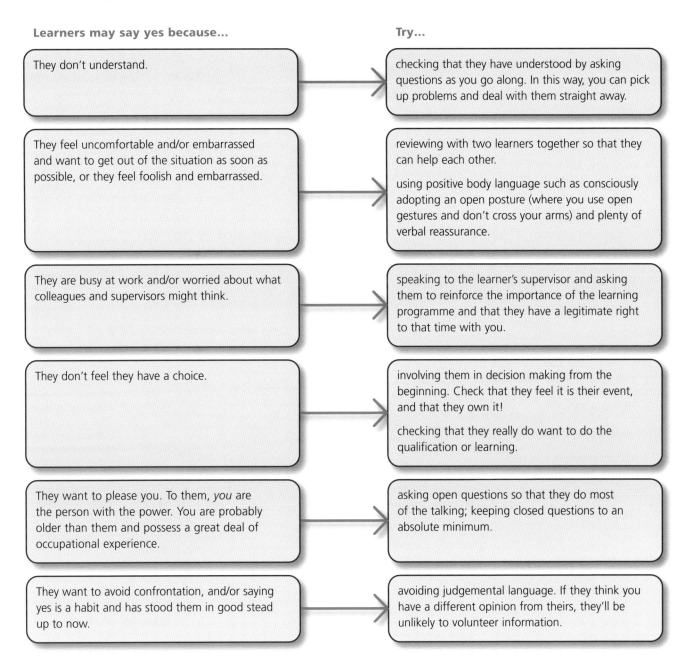

Learners may say yes because...

Try...

Learners may say yes because...	Try...
They don't understand.	checking that they have understood by asking questions as you go along. In this way, you can pick up problems and deal with them straight away.
They feel uncomfortable and/or embarrassed and want to get out of the situation as soon as possible, or they feel foolish and embarrassed.	reviewing with two learners together so that they can help each other. using positive body language such as consciously adopting an open posture (where you use open gestures and don't cross your arms) and plenty of verbal reassurance.
They are busy at work and/or worried about what colleagues and supervisors might think.	speaking to the learner's supervisor and asking them to reinforce the importance of the learning programme and that they have a legitimate right to that time with you.
They don't feel they have a choice.	involving them in decision making from the beginning. Check that they feel it is their event, and that they own it! checking that they really do want to do the qualification or learning.
They want to please you. To them, *you* are the person with the power. You are probably older than them and possess a great deal of occupational experience.	asking open questions so that they do most of the talking; keeping closed questions to an absolute minimum.
They want to avoid confrontation, and/or saying yes is a habit and has stood them in good stead up to now.	avoiding judgemental language. If they think you have a different opinion from theirs, they'll be unlikely to volunteer information.

Sample mid-term review

On the next page is part of a review that took place towards the middle of a three-year apprenticeship. It includes a variety of activities and shows the learner:

- choosing optional units and setting new learning targets
- assembling evidence to do with core units that he has completed, and planning assessment
- facing up to the reasons why he hasn't achieved an important target and arranging for some help.

PROGRESS REVIEW RECORD

Name (print):
DAVE WILLIAMS

Reviewer (print):
SARAH TAYLOR

Date:
29 April 2005

Date of last review:
3 February 2005

Last review used at this review?
Yes

If not why not?
N/A

Contributors: College tutor ☑   Workplace supervisor ☑   Other ☐

> This is written by Dave, the learner, who gives his own opinion about how well he's progressing in discussion with his reviewer. From here, you can clarify where targets need to be set and modified.

HOW ARE YOU DOING?

1   I've finished my off-job training and I think I did well to get 100% attendance record. I've achieved my learning targets but haven't got all my evidence for assessment together yet. I need to set myself a target to do this.

2   I've collected examples of telephone messages that I've taken, fax header sheets, fax report sheets, and the organisational procedures that I use when telephoning and faxing (Unit 203). I've also kept a copy of the document with handwritten amendments that I copied and entered into the computer (Unit 204). I think I could be assessed for these units.

3   I want to learn how to carry out automated tasks on our company's computer system and how to use the software.

4   I've chosen these optional units: 205 Record, store and supply information using a paper-based filing system, 207 Provide effective customer service and 213 Support the use of information technology.

5   I want to finish my communication key skill. I'm not good at report writing and I've been avoiding doing it.

> Here, the reviewer has summarised feedback from Dave's employer and key skills tutor. You could also invite them to participate in the review process and give feedback directly to the learner.

EMPLOYER'S COMMENTS

Bill is pleased with Dave's progress generally and sees improvements in his communication skills. He mentioned his telephone manner and was impressed at the way Dave dealt with a potential conflict with a customer last week.

TUTOR COMMENTS

Cathy (Dave's key skills tutor) thinks he is ready to attempt the tests. She thinks he may need help with report writing as he didn't complete the course assignment.

WHICH OF YOUR SMART TARGETS HAVE YOU ACHIEVED FROM LAST TIME?

Achieved	Not achieved	Why not?	Subsequent plans
All targets to do with my core training and mandatory units (see previous review)	Write a report of 400-500 words	Being too busy and avoiding it.	I have asked Elaine, the office manager, to supervise and help me.

> Progress towards targets agreed at the last review form the basis of this one. It's helpful to have them in front of you.

> In this example, Dave is honest about why he hasn't made progress in one area. This is because he has a good relationship with his reviewer and is confident about assessing his own progress.

SMART TARGETS FOR NEXT PERIOD

What are you going to do?	By when	What help will you need?	Who will do this? Have they agreed?
1 Write a report of 400–500 words, with correct punctuation, about how I deal with telephone enquiries from customers and how I ring customers when their orders come in.	14 May 2005	Help with structuring and headings	Cathy – key skills tutor. Not yet
		Someone to check my spelling and punctuation	Elaine. Yes
2 Learn how to use the company's XYZ software package and accurately carry out input, transfer and summation tasks unsupervised on at least three occasions	29 July 2005	Support from Bill (manager)	Bill. Yes
3 Put all remaining evidence for the mandatory units in the portfolio	Date to be agreed with assessor	None	Gary. Not yet.

ADDITIONAL NOTES/INFORMATION

Dave may have to go into hospital in the autumn. Dates for his key skills tests need to be arranged for June/July if possible.

Here, anything else that might affect Dave's learning or achievement is identified.

ACTION PLAN

Action points	By when	What help will you need?	Who
1 Arrange to meet Gary Bates (assessor) and plan next assessment	21 May 2005	None	Dave
2 Arrange to be shown how to use company software.	14 May 2005	None	Dave
3 Contact Cathy and arrange for a key skills coaching session and dates for tests (see additional notes above).	14 May 2005	None	Sarah
4 Start an evidence file for the optional units	14 May 2005	None	Dave

Notice how the action points come naturally as a result of reviewing progress towards specific targets.

Date of next review: 29 July 2005

Agreed by:

Apprentice Sign: Dave Williams   Print: DAVE WILLIAMS

Reviewer Sign: Sarah Taylor   Print: SARAH TAYLOR

Planning future learning

Towards the end of learners' programmes, you will begin to look ahead to the future. In these final sessions, concentrate on:

- identifying gaps in learning or evidence collection

- taking urgent remedial action in areas where learners need help with their learning and development

- continuing to plan for summative assessment

- summarising achievements and arranging for certification, where appropriate

- planning future learning and development – making the learning to learn skills more visible and talking about how they can continue using them to become independent learners.

'I hated reviews to start with. I found it really difficult and couldn't see the point of it. I just wanted to get on with the job. But my reviewer helped me think about how I was doing and so did my supervisor. I started to see how it all came together. One way was my approach to learning things. It changed completely. I started off learning everything by doing and making mistakes. I didn't want anything to do with reading or or e-learning or anything like that. Then I went on a leadership course and they told me I was good at it. I came back and started studying for a supervisory qualification and I used the Internet and some self-study modules. I could see how trying out different ways of learning worked for me and I wasn't afraid to give it a try. It doesn't worry me any more, and it definitely would have done in the past.

Learner

Thinking about thinking

The ability to reflect on one's own thinking processes and strategies and to consciously change these is known as metacognition. There are three basic elements involved: developing a plan of action; monitoring the plan; and evaluating its effectiveness. These are the elements that underpin the review process, and using them will help the learner develop metacognition.

At the end of learners' programmes, you might also consider evaluating the success of the review process as far as the learner is concerned. This will give both you and your organisation valuable information concerning the success of the learning process itself. It's also a good time to concentrate on the skills of reflection and learning and to discuss these with the learner so that they know their approaches to tackling new tasks and learning and feel equipped to deal with new challenges when they leave you.

Turn to the section on quality assurance on page 75 more information on evaluating the review process.

3 The reviewer's toolkit

In your role as a reviewer you'll need a range of skills and techniques. This part of the guide looks at each of the main areas of expertise required, which you can refer to according to your needs at different times. You don't have to work through it sequentially. Use it as a reminder or as a reference tool when you need help with a particular topic.

The subjects covered here are:

- *setting targets*

- *encouraging reflection*

- *giving feedback*

- *action planning*

- *recording progress*

- *tracking progress*

- *quality assurance.*

Setting targets

One of the most important skills you'll need as a reviewer is the ability to help learners set their own targets. Targets tell you and your learner exactly what they are aiming for, and why. By looking at progress towards targets, learners can see how far they've come, and you can then help them modify their targets or set new ones as appropriate. Good targets break down learning into a series of small, measurable steps that can form the basis of discussion during reviews.

It is not always easy to set effective and appropriate targets, and you need to understand the target-setting process yourself before you can expect learners to take an active part in negotiating their learning with you. This section discusses the different types of learning target and takes you through the process of target setting step by step. A series of short activities towards the end of the section (pages 48–9) will enable you to test your knowledge.

What the standards say

Unit L16 Monitor and review progress with learners

You need to be able to:

- identify new learning needs and objectives.

You need to show that you have general knowledge and understanding of:

- how to set and renegotiate learning objectives.

Taxonomies of learning

Taxonomies of learning are a useful tool when target setting, for both tutors and learners. Tutors can use the cues a learner gives them to set learning targets and to design learning and assessment at the appropriate level for that learner. Similarly, learners can determine the level of questions being set in exams or tests and use the cues to improve their learning skills.

Benjamin Bloom created a taxonomy (or hierarchy) for categorising the level of abstraction in questions commonly used by educators. This taxonomy is concerned with the cognitive domain, that is, knowledge and understanding. It starts with the concrete – knowing and remembering facts – and moves on to more complex and abstract skills such as the ability to analyse and synthesise information, through to evaluation. There are other taxonomies of learning, but Bloom's is widely recognised.

The following table[4] shows the main categories, with examples of skills you would expect the learner to demonstrate and the kinds of things to look for at each stage.

---

4   From Benjamin S. Bloom et al, *Taxonomy of educational objectives*. Published by Allyn and Bacon, Boston, MA. Copyright © 1984 by Pearson Education. Adapted by permission of the publisher.

Bloom's taxonomy

Category	Skills you would expect the learner to demonstrate
1 Knowledge	knowledge and recall of events, places or dates, major ideas, subject matter **Look for:** list, examine, tell, show, label, describe, who, why, what, when, etc.
2 Understanding	grasping meaning; translating knowledge into a new context interpreting facts; comparing and contrasting inferring causes and predicting consequences **Look for:** interpret, discuss, predict, summarise, associate, estimate.
3 Application	using information, methods, theories and concepts in new situations solving problems using required skills or knowledge **Look for:** demonstrate, apply, discover, experiment, show, classify, calculate, illustrate.
4 Analysis	seeing patterns and identifying components recognising hidden meanings **Look for:** explain, infer, compare, select, classify, arrange.
5 Synthesis	using old ideas to create new ones; generalising from given facts relating knowledge from several areas, predicting and drawing conclusions **Look for:** What if...?, integrate, modify, rewrite, generalise, substitute, plan, invent, design.
6 Evaluation	comparing and discriminating between ideas assessing value making choices based on reasoned argument verifying the value of evidence recognising subjectivity **Look for:** assess, decide, recommend, conclude, summarise, convince, judge, support, grade, test, measure.

Different types of learning target

It's easier to set learning targets in some areas than others, and you'll need to give some thought to sequencing your targets in a logical way. Taxonomies of learning can be helpful here: for example, you wouldn't set a target that required your learner to analyse or synthesise information before they had grasped the basics of the subject.

During the early stages you will be setting targets with learners to enable them to learn the skills they need and acquire any associated knowledge. The skills and knowledge often go together, as with these two targets:

1 *Know what all the function keys on a PC are for.*

2 *Be able to use the function keys on a PC appropriately.*

The first target is to do with knowing and the second about doing: you need the first in order to do the second properly.

A third area where you may need to set targets is to do with having the right approach. It's more difficult to set targets when trying to change people's behaviour. For example, the following target assumes that the learner can adopt the right behaviour when dealing with customers:

Deal with customer complaints using company procedures to the customer's satisfaction.

A fearful learner who lacks confidence with customers couldn't achieve this target. You would first have to set them a target that concerns their behaviour with customers. For example:

Adopt an assertive approach when dealing with customer complaints.

If your learner has a learning need in this area, even this target doesn't tell them enough about how to achieve this. You would also need to set them some more specific learning targets, such as:

1 *Practise using the company greeting and a suitable opening question with all customers under supervision by 13 July.*

2 *List five open questions and five follow-up questions and use them to determine customers' needs under supervision by next Friday.*

3 *Identify three situations where referral to a higher authority is appropriate.*

4 *Learn to identify my own feelings and use breathing techniques to keep these in check when dealing with the next customer complaint under supervision.*

Self-check: analysing targets

Look at the following targets. Decide if they are to do with knowledge, skill or attitude, or a mixture.

1 *Convert units of measurement from metric to imperial with all calculations accurate.*

2 *Use the company greeting when answering the telephone to the customer's satisfaction.*

3 *Get to the training centre on time every day for the next three weeks.*

Answers: *1 is about knowledge; 2 concerns knowledge and attitude; 3 is mainly about attitude to work.*

Look at this target and the way in which it has been modified over time. What's the logical order?

1 *Collect evidence of written communications that use full stops and punctuation correctly.*

2 *Learn how to use full stops and capital letters correctly in all written communications.*

3 *Use full stops and capital letters correctly in all written communications.*

Answer: *2, 3, 1. Learners need to learn things first, then practise them, and lastly be summatively assessed when they have met their target and can perform the task to the standard in question.*

Steps to target setting

You may find it helpful to take these steps when setting targets with learners:

1 Check motivation

Before you start, be clear about why your learner wants to learn something. Compare these two examples. In your opinion, which learner is more likely to succeed?

'This month everyone in our department has to learn how to carry out a stock check electronically for our year end.'

'I'd like to learn how to touch type – I know my speed will increase.'

The answer is the second one. All learners have to learn things they don't particularly want to, but they are more likely to succeed if their reasons for learning are positive ones.

2 Set goals

Goals are general statements of intent, purpose and direction. They are broad aims, to be reached after a relatively long period (weeks, months or even years), and can be achieved in a variety of ways. A goal summarises in a sentence what the learner wants to learn, achieve or change. Examples of long-term 'life' goals are:

- to get a job

- to become an accountant

- to gain Level 3 NVQ.

Learners will, of course, have goals such as these, but they are too broad for the purposes of reviewing. You need to break them down into smaller steps. For example, 'to get a job' might mean the learner has to learn how to:

- get an interview for a job

- write a job application letter

- turn up on time for work regularly.

The goals chosen will reflect the needs of the individual learner. Your skills as a reviewer will enable you respond to your particular learner and set the right target at the right level, and at the right time for the learner.

3 Set targets

You will need to break goals down into even smaller steps for learning purposes, especially if a number of skills or tasks is involved. For example, 'to write a job application letter' involves being able to:

- use the right punctuation

- set out a letter

- use correct spelling

- write in sentences

- use paragraphs correctly

- use appropriate language and expressions.

If the learner has a skills need in this area, you may have to select some or all of these targets.

4 Select a realistic target

A realistic target will stretch your learner while also being within their reach. This means that your targets for learning will be specific to the individual learner, and their needs and circumstances. You can check whether your target is realistic by asking the following questions:

- Is the learner capable of achieving it?

- Is it relevant to their job and/or to their life generally?

- Do they have the opportunity to learn or practise it?

- Are the resources available?

- Is the support available?

- Do the learner's circumstances (their personal or work life) point to them achieving it?

If you answer no to any of these questions, you may have to set a different target.

5 Set a time limit

You need to decide with your learner how long it will take them to achieve their target. Sometimes their circumstances mean that they have to achieve it within a certain time, as in these examples:

'I need to learn how to carry out stock-taking procedures by 31 March. This is the end of our financial year.'

'Learn how to give mouth-to-mouth resuscitation and heart massage by 15 June. Everyone working on site has to do a first-aid course and this is the date of the practical exam.'

If there's no imposed time limit, it's important to agree one with the learner. One way is to use the dates you set for your review meetings, but make sure you take account of busy periods and the learner's motivation. You may need to adjust timings and check progress between reviews if your learner is struggling or unmotivated.

6 Set measures

Learners need to know when they've done enough to achieve their target and that what they've done is acceptable. This means including some kind of measure within your target, for example:

'when I've got an interview'

'with no mistakes'

'when my manager tells me I've got it right'

'dealing with five customers to their satisfaction.'

SMART targets

You may find the SMART acronym helpful when setting targets with learners. Use the table below to check that your targets are smart when you are reviewing with learners.

SMART stands for...	This means...
Specific	You state exactly what the learner will do or learn.
Measurable	How will the learner, you, or the assessor know when they've achieved it? There needs to be a concrete, measurable outcome so that it's clear when the target has been met.
Achievable	The target should be challenging but not too difficult for the learner.
Relevant	The target needs to be relevant to the learner and move them towards their goal. (If they cannot see the point of the target they are unlikely to bother with it.) Opportunities for learning and practice, support needs and resources should also be available.
Time bound	You give a date by which the target will be achieved. Try to be as specific as possible.

SMARTER targets mean targets can also be:

Enjoyable and **R**ewarding.

These are to do with maintaining learners' motivation to learn. If you want learners to become proficient at managing their own learning and performance, it's important to involve them in the target-setting process so that their learning is a positive experience.

Talking targets with learners

Here are some pointers for setting goals and targets when you're with learners:

- Start by asking learners the reasons why they've joined the programme or want to learn. They'll give you their 'life' goals, like: 'To be a nurse' or 'To do my apprenticeship.'

- Avoid using unit titles from NVQs as learning targets. These are too broad. Think smaller – and start with what your learner needs to learn first. You can then use element titles and performance criteria as the basis for practising and applying knowledge and skills once they have been learnt.

- Familiarise learners with the procedure for setting targets before you explain SMART or use it as a checking tool yourself.

'I don't want to know about the theory. Tell me they're SMART targets later. Show me what one is and how to set one first.'
Learner

- If the learner is employed or carrying out a job, start by listing the tasks they need to be good at and set targets in each of these areas. You can use their job description as a starting point.

'An important part of my job is dealing with customer orders over the telephone. One of the things I have to know is how to convert decimal to imperial measurements as our customers and suppliers use both. I only learnt decimals so I need to set myself a target in this area.'
Learner

- If the target seems unclear or daunting to the learner, it's probably too big. Break it down into smaller steps and set a separate target for each area you identify.

- Similarly, be prepared to set manageable targets when learners are acquiring new skills or tackling new situations.

'I set myself a target to learn five new words a week and to use them. I could see my spelling was getting better.'
Learner

Self-check: setting good targets

Writing good targets takes time and practice. Here are five self-check activities to help you.

Activity 1

Look at the list of objectives below. Tick the ones you think are goals and those you think are targets.

	Goal	Target
1 To collect evidence for unit 3	☐	☐
2 Carry out one review with each of six learners before Friday 10 June 2005	☐	☐
3 Achieve Unit L16 Monitor and review progress with learners by the end of December	☐	☐
4 Improve my timekeeping by being at work at least five minutes before 8.30am every day for the week beginning 10 June 2005	☐	☐
5 To work faster and be more reliable	☐	☐

(Answers: 1. Goal, 2. Target, 3. Goal, 4.Target, 5.Goal)

Activity 2

Now look at the list of targets below and decide which are specific and which are not.

Target	Specific? Yes	No
1 Accurately complete all the boxes of the September 2005 VAT return	☐	☐
2 Improve my timekeeping	☐	☐
3 Practise spelling	☐	☐
4 Check goods delivered against delivery notes and accurately list missing items	☐	☐
5 Complete an evidence matrix in my portfolio for all six items of evidence relating to Unit 2.1	☐	☐

(Answers: 1.Yes, 2. No, 3.No, 4.Yes, 5.Yes.)

Activity 3

Which of these targets do you think are measurable?

Target	Measurable? Yes	No
1 Collect examples of materials that you use next week	☐	☐
2 Start collecting evidence towards Unit 4.1	☐	☐
3 Practise using the till	☐	☐
4 Serve red and white wine to table 3 to the customers' satisfaction	☐	☐
5 Show four new employees how to use the electronic clocking-in system until they are all confident to use it	☐	☐

(Answers: 1.No, 2. No, 3.No, 4.Yes, 5.Yes.)

Activity 4

Now decide which of the following targets are time-bound and which are not.

Target	Time-bound?	
	Yes	No
1 Ask your manager to show you how to use a spreadsheet package	☐	☐
2 Prepare vegetables for the next few shifts	☐	☐
3 Complete unit CR3.1 before 30 June 2005	☐	☐
4 Achieve key skills at Level 1	☐	☐
5 Use your spare time to learn how to use a keyboard	☐	☐

(Answers: 1.No, 2. No, 3.Yes, 4.No, 5.No.)

Activity 5

Look at these targets and decide whether or not they meet each of the SMART criteria by ticking the appropriate columns.

Target	S	M	A	R	T
Follow the procedure and carry out the powered tools pre-start inspection on the hammer drill, completing the documentation accurately, five times before 10 August 2005	☐	☐	☐	☐	☐
Begin Units CR01 and CRO2 before May	☐	☐	☐	☐	☐
Put in more effort when asked to do tasks by the manager	☐	☐	☐	☐	☐
Practise numerically filing customer orders before the next review	☐	☐	☐	☐	☐
Provide examples of three construction materials used this week	☐	☐	☐	☐	☐
Provide evidence towards Unit CR02.3 by 28 May 2004	☐	☐	☐	☐	☐

Answers:

Target	S	M	A	R	T
Follow the procedure and carry out the powered tools pre-start inspection on the hammer drill, completing the documentation accurately, five times before 10 August 2005	x	x	x	x	x
Begin Units CR01 and CRO2 before May	o	o	x	x	o
Put in more effort when asked to do tasks by the manager	o	o	x	o	o
Practise numerically filing customer orders before the next review	o	o	x	x	o
Provide examples of three construction materials used this week	x	x	X	x	o
Provide evidence towards Unit CR02.3 by 28 May 2004	o	o	x	x	x

Now go back over your answers and reflect on your own skills in setting goals and targets. Is there anything you find difficult? If so, do you need to set yourself a SMART target in this area?

If you do, write it down here:

Using plain English

When writing targets, you must make sure that you and your learner both understand what you mean. There's a temptation to become wordy or complicated if you're trying to fulfil all the SMART criteria. Here are some points to bear in mind when setting targets with learners:

- Agree the target with your learner first. If you want to use SMART, use it as a guide to check what you've both written. Add any details at this stage.

- Don't be afraid to use the learner's words or language. Involve them in writing their own targets and try to keep the process at their level.

- Keep it short and simple. If you find yourself writing a long target, ask whether you can set two or three smaller ones instead.

- Make sure that the learner understands the targets you have set. Ask them to explain what they'll be doing and be prepared to change the targets if they don't understand them.

Setting deadlines

People vary in their approaches to learning and may have different ways of tackling deadlines. If we don't understand our learners, particularly in relation to setting goals and targets, then it's hardly surprising if they don't do what we expect them to do.

The Myers-Briggs personality type indicator

In the 1950s Katherine Cook Briggs and her daughter Isabel Briggs Myers studied the work of the Swiss psychoanalyst Carl G. Jung (1875–1961). Essentially, Jung suggested that we all have preferred ways of doing things. It doesn't mean that we can't do things differently; it's just that we find it easier to do them in one way rather than another. He developed a theory that there are four basic psychological traits and that people have them in varying proportions, and this determines the way they deal with the world. Briggs and Myers developed Jung's theory of psychological types into a personality model and questionnaire, which has since become one of the most widely used questionnaires in the world. Its aim is to enable individuals from all backgrounds to understand their own and others' personalities, in order to appreciate differences between people and avoid misunderstanding and miscommunication.[5]

Try this:

Do you normally eat using a knife in your right hand and a fork in your left? Try swapping them over the next time you eat. You will be able to manage to eat this way but it will take more concentration and the food may be cold before you've finished! If this is true for you, then you can safely say that using the knife in your right hand is your preference.

Similarly, everyone has their own preferences about how to meet deadlines. Some people will complete work long before a deadline, while others prefer to leave things till the last minute. The former (called 'judgers', although this doesn't mean they are judgemental) are generally organised, methodical and systematic and want to avoid the stress that they experience from having to do things at the last minute. The latter ('perceivers', although again it doesn't mean they are perceptive) prefer to be spontaneous, flexible, enjoy change and feel energised by last-minute pressures.

We will all be somewhere between the two extremes, and the key to getting learners to meet deadlines is to try and establish their *preferred* approach.

Remember...

If your personality type and preferred style is the opposite of the learner's and you don't adjust your approach to match their preferred option, misunderstandings about what is to be done, and by when, are likely.

---

5   *Introduction to type, A guide to understanding your results*, Isabel Briggs Myers, revised by Linda K. Kirby and Katherine D. Myers, OPP Ltd., Oxford 2000. ISBN 1 85639 067 5.

For 'judgers', targets for achievement could:	For 'perceivers', targets for achievement could:
be less frequent	be more frequent
include many tasks	include fewer tasks
be very structured, clearly stating how they are to be achieved	be open and flexible in the planning of how they are to be achieved

To make this work for learners you first must understand yourself. If, for example, you err towards the side of the judgers, you are likely to be clear about what you want the learner to do. You may even write them a list or sequence about what to do. If you prefer to take the perceiver approach you are likely to leave things much more to the learner.

Self-check: judger or perceiver?

This is not a scientifically constructed questionnaire and so the results are not absolute, but it will help you begin to understand yourself and your learners.[6]

1 Think about the last time you had some important work to be done by a specific date. Did you:

   a start as soon as you could so as to leave some time to spare? ☐

   or

   b start when you had just enough time to complete it? ☐

2 If you are asked to do a project, do you prefer:

   a many guidelines? ☐

   or

   b few guidelines? ☐

3 When you download your emails do you:

   a Reply to those that need a reply immediately? ☐

   or

   b Reply to some and do the others at intervals throughout the day? ☐

4 In your diary, do you prefer to have:

   a Lots of fixed appointments and activities planned? ☐

   or

   b Few fixed appointments and activities planned? ☐

5 If you had planned to go to the cinema with a friend this weekend and they cancelled at the very last minute, would you:

   a be irritated? ☐

   or

   b welcome the opportunity to find something else to do? ☐

If you have answered mostly (a)s then you are probably a 'judger'. If you have answered mostly (b)s then you are likely to be a 'perceiver'. If you have a balance of both, you may not have a strong preference for either approach.

You could use the above questions as the basis for a discussion with learners about deadlines. Whatever you do, don't turn it into a test, as your results will not be reliable or valid. (See *Excellence in initial assessment* for more information on reliable and valid tests.) However, the results may help you to structure and plan activities towards meeting targets.

6 If you want to use a well-constructed questionnaire, the Myers Briggs Type Inventory published by OPP Ltd., Oxford, may be suitable.

Encouraging reflection

Reviewing as a development process means encouraging learners to reflect on their progress. This means not just checking whether or not they carried out the tasks you've agreed with them, but also getting them to think about how and why they tackled their learning and what they got out of it. Your job is to get them to think more deeply about their learning and performance. Reflection is a skill in its own right, and encouraging learners to develop this skill will enhance their ability to think critically about themselves, their working environment and their learning. You're also equipping them to think on their feet and helping them to take charge of their own learning when they leave you.

Further benefits for learners are:

- they discover that they can learn from their mistakes – and that a mistake doesn't necessarily mean they've failed

- they gradually take ownership of their own learning

- they can be objective about their own feelings and reactions

- they can begin to understand their own patterns of behaviour and approaches to learning

- critically reflecting eventually enables learners to question wider assumptions and ask questions like: Why do we do it this way? What's the organisation trying to achieve? Is this the right job for me?

The reflective practitioner

Donald Schön wrote a series of influential books concerning the development of reflective practitioners, based around what experienced practitioners and professionals actually do. In his book *The Reflective Practitioner* (1983), Schön describes two types of reflection: reflection in action and reflection on action.

Reflection in action is about thinking creatively 'on your feet' when you're trying to find a way of dealing with a task or situation. When faced with a new or puzzling problem, Schön found that professionals tackled them like this:

- by allowing themselves to feel confused or surprised

- by reflecting critically on the facts before them, their own feelings and any assumptions or accepted practices about how things are done.

This meant they came up with new ways of thinking about and dealing with the problem facing them.

Reflection on action is something you do after an event. Situations where people deal with an emergency, or act out of instinct, or that they find unpleasant and prefer to avoid, can be reflected on after the event with the help of a skilled reviewer.

It can be helpful to bear these ideas in mind with learners, particularly if they are learning from real-life situations such as the workplace. You won't always be there to review with them when something significant takes place, but you can encourage learners themselves to identify and keep a record of key events and to note their response to these events. You can then encourage them to reflect on what happened at the next review session.

What the standards say

Unit L16. Monitor and review progress with learners

You need to be able to:

- encourage learners to express their own views on their own progress

- base your reviews of progress on the views of learners and your assessment of their progress to date.

You need to show that you have general knowledge and understanding of:

- how to involve learners in the review (and assessment) process

- how to put learners at their ease

- how to apply interview and discussion techniques.

Creating rapport with learners

It's important that learners feel relaxed about sharing their thoughts and feelings with you. Part of your job is to create a climate where the learner can reflect freely, and this means building a relationship of trust between the two of you.

Going straight to targets and action points isn't helpful: you need to allow the process of reflection to unfold during your discussions with learners. From their point of view, it may be the first time they've spoken to someone else about what they've been doing. You're helping them see the progress they've made and think critically about how they got there.

Self-check: rapport-building skills

Check your own skills in building rapport by asking a learner you know well to answer the following questions honestly (go on, be brave). Actively seek feedback on your performance by asking them for examples of things you did or didn't do.

When we meet to review your progress...	Yes	No	Example
Do I give you enough time and my full attention?	☐	☐	
Do I encourage you to share your thoughts and feelings?	☐	☐	
Do I make you think about what you've learnt?	☐	☐	
Do I listen to you and pick up on anything important?	☐	☐	
Do I challenge you when you need to be challenged?	☐	☐	
Do you feel as though your thoughts, opinions and feelings count?	☐	☐	
Do you feel relaxed talking to me about your progress?	☐	☐	
Do you feel involved in making decisions about your learning and progress?	☐	☐	
Do you feel confident that anything you say to me will be kept in confidence (unless we both agree otherwise)?	☐	☐	
Do you feel able to ask me questions or challenge me if you don't understand or disagree with something I say?	☐	☐	

Ideally, your learner will have said yes and given you positive examples of things you do. If you have a few 'no' answers or some negative examples, you may want to discuss them with a colleague such as your training manager.

'Reflecting is much more than reviewing. It's when you help the learner to think in depth about an aspect of their performance and get them to understand what happened and why. You're looking for meaning. You need to be a skilled questioner yourself and good at listening and picking up on things the learner says.'

Reviewer

Here are some examples of things you can ask your learner to reflect on:

- **a key incident**, such as: a stock-take; a reorganisation; an accident; a break-in or theft; or taking responsibility for the reception desk (or similar) for the afternoon

- **opportunities** that the learner identifies as important: like sharing the results of a project with their team or doing a presentation to management

- **mistakes**, or a negative learning episode: failing a test; a project that's gone wrong; an interview that didn't result in a job or a machine that's blown up.

The stages of reflection

When helping learners reflect you can go through the process in stages, as shown in the diagram below. Think of these six steps as a framework rather than something to stick to rigidly: you can change the order or miss out a step if appropriate. The final step leads to further reflection, as the process is an iterative one and you repeat the cycle.

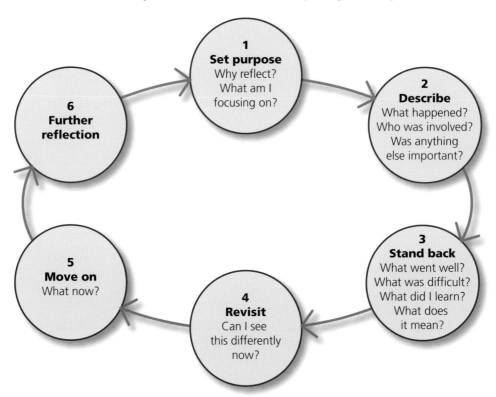

1 Set purpose

Start by agreeing what the learner will reflect on and what you want to achieve. It's helpful to be clear about what you're focusing on and why. Your skills as a reviewer are important here, as you may want to introduce a topic for reflection, particularly if you wish to challenge your learner or if they've skipped over an opportunity for learning.

If the learner doesn't have a purpose, go straight to step two – you'll soon pick up on something they did that you can ask them to reflect on more deeply.

2 Describe

Learners are usually good at describing what's happened, especially if they have used reflective tools like learning logs or diaries. However, real reflection will take them further, using stages 3, 4 and 5. At this describing stage you want them to be able to say more than just what happened and concentrate instead on *how* it happened. Use open and prompt questions to get the full story first, for example:

What happened after that?

Was anyone else there? What did they do?

What equipment did you use?

How did you manage to keep going?

At this stage you need to be listening, and the learner should be doing virtually all the talking with a bit of prompting from you.

3 Stand back

At this stage you can encourage your learner to be objective about what happened. To do this, you need to ask questions that get them to think more critically about what happened, for example:

When you cut the panels out, what was the difficulty?

Sounds like the report went down well. What was good about it?

When you raised your voice during the discussion – what was that like?

Don't be afraid to explore feelings at this point. How learners react in certain situations can provide useful learning points, as in this example:

Q: *So how did you feel when the customer shouted at you?*

A: *Really angry. It took me a while to calm down afterwards.*

Q: *But you said you gave her a refund. Did you shout back at her?*

A: *No. I just followed normal procedures.*

Q: *Will the customer come back, do you think?*

A: *I don't see why not – I didn't do anything to upset her and she went off happy with the refund.*

Q: *Why is it important to keep your feelings under control in a situation like that?*

A: *So that they'll come back and spend more money.*

The key question the reviewer asks is about the importance of keeping feelings under control – it isn't until she asks this question that the learner begins to see that she's done the right thing and understand the reasons why.

You may want to sum up by asking the learner what they think they have learned as a result and – more importantly – how they learned it. They may find this difficult at first, but stick with it. Here's a continuation of the previous example:

Q: *So what have you learned from this situation, do you think?*

A: *How to give a refund?*

Q: *Yes, anything else?*

A: *(silence)*

Q: *What about your feelings?*

A: *Oh, yes. I was angry, but I kept myself under control when I was dealing with a customer who was rude.*

At this point, too, you might encourage learners to make links between what they have learned and ideas or general conclusions they might draw.

'When I reflected on my report and the conclusions I could see how the ideas I'd come up with for our department could apply across the whole organisation. I decided to do a presentation to management.'

Learner

4 Revisit

You may be able to get the learner to see a situation differently, or learn something by looking at it in a different way. Ask:

Can you experiment?

Can you approach the task in a different way?

What about trying a different way of learning?

What you are doing here is being creative and helping the learner deal with uncertainties or unknowns. This is particularly useful if the learner is facing a new situation or has had something go wrong. It's also an ideal way of introducing different approaches to learning if you know the learner could benefit from trying out something new.

5 Move on

At this stage you are aiming for some kind of resolution. It needn't be anything hard and fast but you may need to help the learner reach their own conclusion. Also at this stage, you will begin to identify areas for further action and where targets need to be set or modified.

Think in terms of:

- identifying options and prioritising. If you've been actively listening to your learner you can be extremely effective at this point by summing up what you've heard. For example:

  Listening to you, it seems to me you've got three options: you can go on a course, go through the manual and work it out for yourself, or get your supervisor to show you.

- asking further questions:

  What does this mean?

  What needs to change?

  What would you do differently next time?

- identifying what needs to happen next.

6 Further reflection

When you've planned what happens next, the reflection cycle starts again.

Tools for reflection

You can use a variety of tools to help learners reflect. If you ask them to keep a record of anything significant as they go along, you then have the basis for discussion when you meet.

Opposite are two different formats to get you started. You can adapt them according to your learners' preferences. The first is a straightforward log; the second gives more scope for personal reflection.

Learning log

Date	What happened?	What I learned

Reflective diary

Date
What happened?
Why I want to reflect on this:
What did I do?
What did other people do?
What resources did I use?
What were the outcomes?
Why did I act as I did?
How do I feel about it?
How have others reacted?
What could I have done differently?
What influenced me?
What have I learned?
What could I do differently next time?
What needs to happen next?

'We concentrate on the learning process when we review. We have two questions: "What are you planning to do over the next 12 weeks?" and "How will you learn this?" Learners write down what happens as they go, to help review their progress and learning against their plans.'

Training manager

Remember…

The earlier you can involve learners in the reviewing process, the more likely they are to be committed to achieving their goals. You can ask learners to:

- write down or key in the results of the review themselves
- customise or design their own review sheets or formats
- communicate the results of reviews with their supervisor, employer or tutor.

Giving feedback

Giving learners specific feedback enables them to see the progress they have made. Feedback in the reviewing context means telling the learner how well they are doing in relation to the targets you have set.

The purpose of giving feedback as part of the review is:

- for the learner to know how well they are doing
- for you to know how well the learner is doing
- to provide you both with the basis for planning what happens next.

What the standards say

Unit L16 Monitor and review progress with learners

You need to be able to:

- give learners positive feedback.

You need to show that you have general knowledge and understanding of:

- how to give learners constructive feedback
- how to put learners at their ease.

Principles of effective feedback

The way in which you give feedback – choosing a suitable time and place – is as important as the feedback itself. You need an environment that supports the feedback process, and the review setting is ideal.

'It's not easy to give feedback. I used to think of it as something to be done as quickly and as painlessly as possible, but this was before I had some training myself. When we role-played and I was on the receiving end of some feedback, I realised that ten minutes in the canteen wasn't going to cut it.'

Trainer

Giving specific feedback means being:

- **objective:** using concrete evidence of the learner's progress such as observations of performance as the basis of any feedback you give
- **specific:** telling the learner exactly where they are performing well and specifying areas where they need to improve
- **non-judgemental:** sticking to the facts and 'owning' what you say
- **prepared:** having evidence of the learner's performance and progress to use as examples
- **skilled:** knowing how to give feedback to learners in a way that doesn't leave them feeling confused or a failure.

How to give feedback

Here are some examples of what to say and when:

1 Start with the positive

You will encourage your learner if you begin by talking about the things that are going well. Start with the general, then move on to the specific. For example:

That's three units of your NVQ you've started. You're doing well. (general)

Your manager tells me you coped with a really difficult customer yesterday. (specific)

I liked the way you introduced the session to the group. (specific)

Compare the two specific examples above with the following:

Your manager tells me you coped with a really difficult customer yesterday. She said you kept calm and gave them a refund.

I liked the way you introduced the session to the group. You explained your objectives and spoke clearly.

You can see from the above specific examples that it is even more helpful to tell the learner exactly what it was they did well. In this way you make progress visible to them.

2 Move on to the negative

Don't be afraid to describe anything the learner is doing wrong or the things that have not gone well. It's how you give your feedback that's important. Compare the following:

You did it wrong. The machine didn't work, did it?

The machine didn't work to start with and you didn't know what to do. What should you have done before switching on?

None of the machines work unless you go through safety procedures first. That's why yours wouldn't start. What will you need to do next time?

All are ways of giving negative feedback, but if you just state facts as in the first example without getting the learner to reflect on what may have gone wrong, you are unlikely to inspire confidence in the long term. Using concrete examples makes it a lot easier for the learner to relate to when they got it wrong, and it makes your job easier because you can be objective.

Remember...

Negative experiences can be turned into opportunities for learning.

3 Involve the learner

This means inviting comment from them as you give feedback. For example:

There isn't a conclusions section on in your report. You've summed up your research findings, but you don't draw conclusions as a result. Did you forget this bit? Or do you need a bit more help?

The feedback you give may seem straightforward to you, particularly if you are an expert in the subject or occupation. However, the learner is just that – a learner. They need time to assimilate information. Ways of doing this include asking them check questions, getting them to summarise what you have said and inviting them to comment.

4 Discuss what happens next

When the learner has understood and agreed with your specific feedback, you can talk about the next stage. You can now modify any targets that may already have been set (in the light of the progress made), and set new ones where there is an obvious learning need.

When things go wrong

Here are some examples of things that may go wrong during a review and suggestions for what you might do or ask:

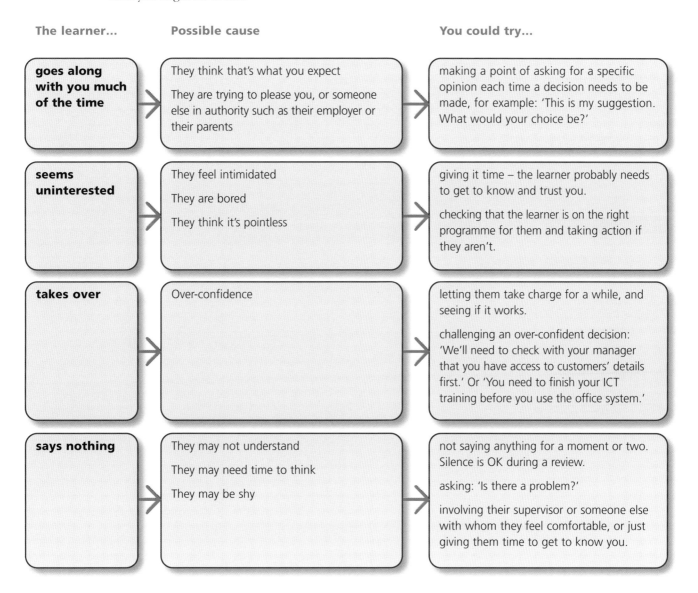

The learner...	Possible cause	You could try...
goes along with you much of the time	They think that's what you expect They are trying to please you, or someone else in authority such as their employer or their parents	making a point of asking for a specific opinion each time a decision needs to be made, for example: 'This is my suggestion. What would your choice be?'
seems uninterested	They feel intimidated They are bored They think it's pointless	giving it time – the learner probably needs to get to know and trust you. checking that the learner is on the right programme for them and taking action if they aren't.
takes over	Over-confidence	letting them take charge for a while, and seeing if it works. challenging an over-confident decision: 'We'll need to check with your manager that you have access to customers' details first.' Or 'You need to finish your ICT training before you use the office system.'
says nothing	They may not understand They may need time to think They may be shy	not saying anything for a moment or two. Silence is OK during a review. asking: 'Is there a problem?' involving their supervisor or someone else with whom they feel comfortable, or just giving them time to get to know you.

Self-check: development needs

Use the space below to reflect on your own development needs when giving feedback on progress.

Do I...	Yes, and I can prove it	No	Not sure
give specific feedback to learners on their progress?		☐	☐
give effective positive feedback to learners?		☐	☐
discuss what went wrong and see what can be learnt from this?		☐	☐
give objective feedback?		☐	☐
involve the learner in the feedback process?		☐	☐
use evidence of performance (such as observations) to inform feedback?		☐	☐

You are aiming to answer yes in all cases. If you aren't sure, or you can't prove it, you may need to set yourself a development target. Use the space below for this.

Development target:

Action planning

Action planning is the last step in the review process. If you've reviewed progress and set targets you'll find it easy to go back over your discussion and specify any further action to be taken. At the end of each review you should record action points – who needs to do what by when – so that you and the learner both know what to do next. Looking at action points can be a useful place to begin the next review: by looking at whether or not everything that was agreed has actually been done.

How to action plan

Action points are the things that need to happen if learners are to achieve their targets. They include the practical steps you'll need to take, such as:

- arranging for learning to take place

- talking to key people such as managers or trainers

- making sure that equipment and resources are available.

Overall, you should aim to answer the following questions:

1   What needs to happen next?

2   Who needs to do it?

3   When does it need to happen?

4   What resources or equipment are needed and how will they be accessed or obtained?

You may need to give the learner time to mull things over before action planning. If you run out of time, agree an action point with the learner around 'identifying options' or 'talking it over with your supervisor' – but follow it up with them over the phone or arrange for your next review to take place shortly.

- Don't be afraid to set action points around interpersonal skills or approaches. This can help to make progress visible and concrete for the learner in these areas.

- Be specific and clear about who's doing what – and make sure your learner agrees to it before you record anything.

- Check that you include key people when deciding who does what. Don't leave it to the learner to negotiate resources and opportunities with senior people unless they are competent and confident to do so. Be prepared to act on your learner's behalf.

- Plan your next review around the targets and action points you've agreed with the learner. Don't just set a date for three months' time because that's standard practice.

From targets to action points

Targets contain implicit actions. For example, the target 'Use the company's software package to process this month's invoices without making any mistakes by 13 September' may lead to a variety of action points, like:

- arranging a coaching session

- liaising with the office manager for the learner to do the task

- asking someone within the company to supervise.

The detail will depend upon the learner's circumstances and the people or resources available.

From reflection to action

It's not always simple to translate reflection into action. Sometimes a learner may need to stop doing something or to think about a task in a different light. However, if you both think it's important, you may want to turn this into something concrete that the learner can do.

'We have women returners in our care homes and they often lack confidence, even though they usually have very good people skills. I've started including things like "Write down at least five things I feel good about between now and the next time we meet." I find turning it into something they have to do makes it real and helps them see what they're good at.'

Reviewer, care

Here's a reminder of the reflection process:

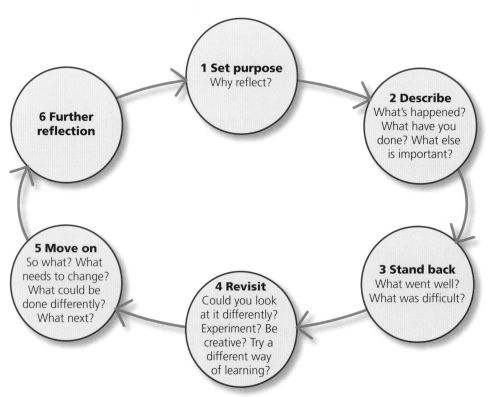

'I use "What?", "So what?" and "Now what?" when I'm reviewing with learners.'

Trainer

Action points will suggest themselves at the revisiting and moving on stages. For example:

'When I reviewed my project I could see from the survey results that it had gone down really well on the production line, so I suggested tackling it in a different way for the packaging line. This meant I had to write a new project plan for management, so that was the first action point.' Learner

'I failed my key skills test the first time round. I was gutted because I never did well at school. If it hadn't been for Asif going over what I'd achieved for my portfolio with me and explaining that I could do it again, I'd have walked out there and then. He said let's meet straight away after the test. He knew it would do my head in.'

Learner

Recording action points

There are many ways to record action points. Here is one example, concerning the run-up to one learner giving a presentation:

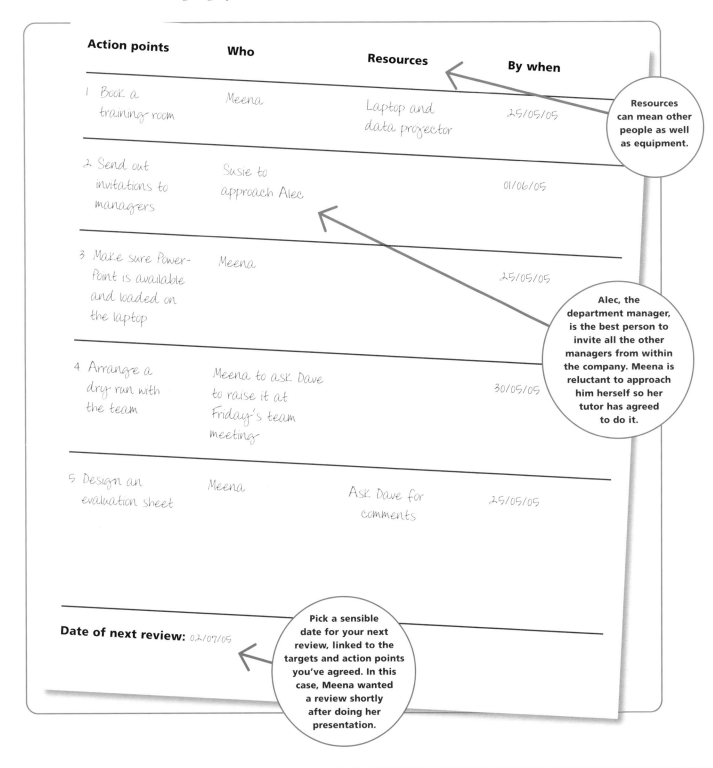

Action points	Who	Resources	By when
1 Book a training room	Meena	Laptop and data projector	25/05/05
2 Send out invitations to managers	Susie to approach Alec		01/06/05
3 Make sure PowerPoint is available and loaded on the laptop	Meena		25/05/05
4 Arrange a dry run with the team	Meena to ask Dave to raise it at Friday's team meeting		30/05/05
5 Design an evaluation sheet	Meena	Ask Dave for comments	25/05/05

Date of next review: 02/07/05

Resources can mean other people as well as equipment.

Alec, the department manager, is the best person to invite all the other managers from within the company. Meena is reluctant to approach him herself so her tutor has agreed to do it.

Pick a sensible date for your next review, linked to the targets and action points you've agreed. In this case, Meena wanted a review shortly after doing her presentation.

Recording progress

The review record is just that – a record. When you're reviewing, your main purpose is to review progress, *not to* complete the form in front of you. Any records you have to complete should facilitate the process, not dictate it. You need to consider carefully, from learners' point of view and as an organisation, what must be documented and what need not be. It helps to have a sense of what you want to cover and the types of questions you are going to ask.

You also need to know where each learner is in relation to the different parts of their programmes – and learners themselves need to know this so that they know how far they've come and what they still have to do. This can be important for maintaining motivation. Ask your learner to bring to the review session the records they have been keeping between reviews (such as learning logs). During your discussions about learning and progress the learner can refer to these as a starting point for active reflection.

Equal opportunities and health and safety

Part of the purpose of reviewing is to check that learners are being treated fairly and are treating others fairly. You also need to ensure that they are working safely and in safe conditions. Learners are often reluctant to divulge information if they think their employer might see what they have said. One way to deal with this is to have a separate sheet to record health and safety and equal opportunities information. These sections are probably best completed by you, the reviewer.

Types of record sheet

You can adapt for your own use the following examples of documentation used to record progress, or use the principles and suggestions to design your own. The first example of a progress review record is for a learner on a long learning programme – in this case a three-year apprenticeship. (The health and safety and equal opportunities record is on a separate sheet.) The second example is more suitable for use on a short course – in this case a 12-hour IT course accessed via the learning resource centre at the workplace.

What the standards say

Unit L16 Monitor and review progress with learners

You need to be able to:

- record, pass on and use the results of the review.

You need to show that you have general knowledge and understanding of:

- how to record and store information for review and assessment purposes

- how to prioritise and summarise information correctly

- how to use information technology to keep records

- how to put information in order

- how to ensure that everyone acts in line with health and safety and environmental protection legislation and best practice

- how to identify and apply relevant legislation to individuals' rights.

What to include

Your record sheet should contain space for:

- **an overview of learning and progress.** This is where you summarise what has been achieved since the last session.

- **progress made against SMART targets.** As a result of talking about progress made, you can modify targets and set new ones. Discuss what has gone well and not so well since the last review, and record any successes and issues. Include strategies that have worked, and use these and the learner's achievements to help you understand their approach to learning as well as to motivate the learner.

- **SMART targets for next period.** You may find it useful to split the writing of these targets into columns, so that you can see that all the SMART criteria have been applied. Decide on deadlines that suit the learner and their preferred learning style. Some people work better with shorter deadlines.

- **progress against long-term goals.** Writing under this heading will show the learner how much they have achieved (and what they still need to do), but don't let it drive the learning process. Learners don't necessarily learn at a steady rate and may become demotivated if they think they haven't achieved much, so make filling in this section as positive as possible.

- **help and support needed.** It is useful to note down here the answers to such questions as:

    Have you struggled with anything since the last review?

    Is there anything stopping you doing your job or getting your NVQ work done?

    Are you worried or concerned about anything?

It's also useful if the record sheet contains prompts and questions to help you and learner make sure that you cover everything necessary. (See also the example on pages 36–7.)

Remember...

When setting targets, you may need to split them into several smaller targets if the learner is starting something new or finding something difficult. Limit targets to one or two topic areas at a time so as not to overwhelm the learner.

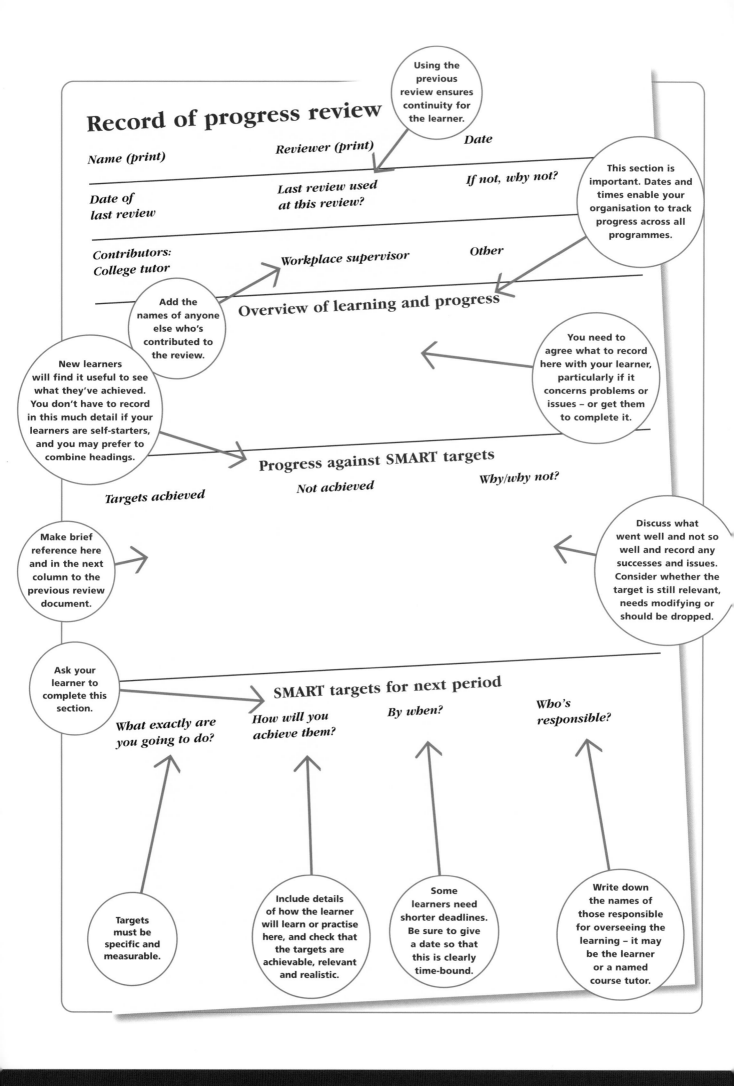

Record of progress review

Using the previous review ensures continuity for the learner.

Name (print)   Reviewer (print)   Date

Date of
last review   Last review used
at this review?   If not, why not?

This section is important. Dates and times enable your organisation to track progress across all programmes.

Contributors:
College tutor   Workplace supervisor   Other

Add the names of anyone else who's contributed to the review.

Overview of learning and progress

You need to agree what to record here with your learner, particularly if it concerns problems or issues – or get them to complete it.

New learners will find it useful to see what they've achieved. You don't have to record in this much detail if your learners are self-starters, and you may prefer to combine headings.

Progress against SMART targets

Targets achieved   Not achieved   Why/why not?

Make brief reference here and in the next column to the previous review document.

Discuss what went well and not so well and record any successes and issues. Consider whether the target is still relevant, needs modifying or should be dropped.

Ask your learner to complete this section.

SMART targets for next period

What exactly are you going to do?   How will you achieve them?   By when?   Who's responsible?

Targets must be specific and measurable.

Include details of how the learner will learn or practise here, and check that the targets are achievable, relevant and realistic.

Some learners need shorter deadlines. Be sure to give a date so that this is clearly time-bound.

Write down the names of those responsible for overseeing the learning – it may be the learner or a named course tutor.

Progress against long-term goals

NVQ Level 2	NVQ Level 3	Technical certificate

This shows learners how far they've come and how much they still need to do.

Key skills/ Basic skills

Communication	Application of number	Information and communication tech.
Working with others	Improving own learning and performance	Problem solving

Action points are concrete things that people need to do. Give specific details of actions that need to be taken. For example: 'Speak to Elaine, Louise's supervisor, and ask her to show Louise how to clean the residents' bathroom.'

Help/support needed

Include changes in personal circumstances, unauthorised absences or unusual behaviour patterns here. Agree with your learner what you will record.

Action plan

What	By when	Resources needed	Who will do this?

Make sure the person concerned has agreed – if not, make it an action point to ask them.

Agreed by:
Apprentice

Signed:

Print:

Employer/supervisor

Signed:

Print:

Reviewer

Signed:

Print:

Date of next review:

Copies of this review will be given to: Learner ☐ Administration Office ☐ College tutor ☐

If you do not wish this information to be shared with the above, please tick box ☐
(Data Protection Act 1998)

By law, you must ensure that your learner knows who will see the review and signs to say they that they agree.

Record of progress – short course

Name (print): EMMA SMITH   **Reviewer (print):** JANE SIMPSON   **Date:** 10 May 2005

PROGRESS TO DATE

I can now turn on the computer, find Microsoft word, enter and edit text, highlight, bold and justify.

It took me a long while to get used to using the mouse instead of just using the arrow keys as I used to when I used a typewriter but I now feel that I have entered the modern world! Can't wait to do more!

PROGRESS TOWARDS PERSONAL TARGETS

Targets achieved	Not achieved	Why not?	Subsequent plans
Enter and edit text Select three formats	Printing documents	The printer is networked and doesn't seem able to cope when we are all trying to print at the same time	The printer is being repaired and I should be able to print next week

Help required / support needed

None required at present

Equal opportunities

Everyone keeps themselves to themselves and I can always get help when I need it.

Health and safety

Jill, the facilitator, checks that we are taking breaks regularly and tells us if we have not adjusted our chairs properly.

Additional notes/ information

SMART TARGETS FOR NEXT PERIOD

What exactly are you going to do?	By when?	What help will you need?	Who will do this/ have they agreed?
Complete the course within the next three visits to the learning resource centre	June 2005	Access to Jill when I need her	N/A

Agreed by:
Learner

Signed: Emma Smith

Print: EMMA SMITH

Tutor/facilitator/reviewer

Signed: Jane Simpson

Print: JANE SIMPSON

Tracking progress

Imagine this:

You have just been on a wonderful two-week holiday. When you unpack you find that you have six loads of washing that need to go in the machine. It seems like a daunting task at first because you know that the drying and ironing come next. But when you have four loads washed, three dry and one ironed, how do you feel then? You are probably fairly pleased and motivated to get the rest finished, and you begin to look forward to a nice drink with your evening meal!

So it is with learners. Your positive feedback about the progress a learner is making will remind them that they are moving towards their goal of completing their learning programme, and this awareness will reward them with a sense of achievement, and motivate them to continue.

Tracking methods

There are various ways to track progress with learners:

- The quantitative method
- The estimation method
- The interval method.

The quantitative method

This is the simplest method, where you create a checklist or matrix of the parts of the course or learning programme and tick them off with learners as you go. For example, you can list the units and elements of an NVQ, key skills and other parts of the apprenticeship. Alternatively, you can break down the learning requirements of qualifications such as the European Computer Driving Licence and tick those as each part is completed. At each review, count up the number of ticks and calculate the percentage achieved as part of the whole.

The estimation method

Here, you and the learner estimate how much they have achieved since the last review. Estimation takes account of progress made over several different aspects of a learning programme at once, even when little is actually finished during any one period. This method is sometimes appropriate for situations where there may be nothing much to report until almost the end of a course or programme, when the learner will suddenly achieve a great deal as they complete many aspects concurrently.

The interval method

Here you break down the learning programme into stages and record progress as learners achieve these stages, or milestones. This method is easy for tutors and assessors to monitor but may make learners feel that they are on a programme for a long time without making much progress. Such learners need confirmation and feedback to maintain their motivation, and this method may be more appropriate for those who are better at motivating themselves.

Using tracking data with learners

Everyone has their preferred way of taking in and processing information. For some learners, calculating a percentage achieved and giving them the figure will work well, but others might need a more graphic interpretation, such as:

- **coloured dots.** Learners can have a checklist or matrix as described above, but use different-coloured dots or stickers to indicate progress. For example, a yellow dot can indicate that they have done some work on that part, they can cover it with another different-coloured dot when almost all that part is complete and finally stick a third coloured dot on top when the part is completed. (Be prepared for some creative and imaginative charts!)

- **graphs.** After a review when you have calculated the percentage, put the data into a spreadsheet and print off a graph comparing last quarter's achievement and the present quarter's achievement towards completion on each aspect of the learning programme.

Learners then have a solid idea of how far they are through their programme and how much they still have to do. This also enables your organisation to spot problems and difficulties before they become a major issue. You can, for example, compare learners making satisfactory progress with those who are not, and explore the reasons before high dropouts occur.

'If you just leave recording to the percentage method you're not practising what you preach in relation to different learning styles. Some, in fact 40 per cent of learners, prefer to take in information visually so just talking about percentages is a cop-out, I think!'

Reviewer

Organisational tracking

It is essential that organisations track and monitor the progress of learners overall. Only by doing this and using this quantitative data can common problems be recognised and remedied and ongoing improvements made. The first stage is to decide on review frequency for each type or group of learners, and set up a database that includes planned review dates and actual review dates. If planned reviews don't occur within a prescribed timescale, action can be taken either to get more staff or to redirect staff to this activity. If learners feel neglected they may well give up and leave. If progress review planning is left to individual members of staff it may not be carried out because all staff have competing demands upon their time.

If a statutory body funds your learning programme you are likely to be contracted to carry out reviews at specific times, and a database is the obvious way to ensure that you comply with contractual requirements.

Questions to ask

You can ask the learner's workplace supervisor, college tutor or mentor similar questions to those you ask the learner concerning progress (see Reviewing in action, page 25) and compare their answers with the learner's. Your discussions should centre round the similarities and differences in how the learner assesses their own progress and how other key contributors say they are progressing.

'Reviewers often don't know what to ask. One ITEC I've worked with has adopted a checklist of questions as prompts for the reviewer and it is working really well. Their reviews have improved and learners' progress has gone up dramatically. Employers can be asked the same or similar questions. This is something I feel very strongly about. If you put lists of questions under headings, it makes QA very clear.' Trainer

Questions should be about any assignments or projects the learner has been involved with; workshops, training courses or college courses they've participated in; and any relevant evidence they've collected. If you're asking a specialist for their opinion, make sure you prepare specific questions in advance. Think in terms of the learner's existing SMART targets and make a list of the things you need to find out.

Here are some general questions to use:

- What can the learner do now that they couldn't three months ago, or at the last review?

- What has gone particularly well? Why?

- What has not gone so well? Why?

- What progress have they made towards their goals and targets?

- Has their attendance been satisfactory? If not, why not?

Here are the questions one reviewer needed to ask her learner's Basic Skills tutor:

1 *Has Hayley been using apostrophes appropriately? Can you give me an example?*

2 *What's she still finding difficult? Does she know when to use capital letters?*

3 *How accurate is Hayley when calculating discounts? We know that she can work out a percentage, but can she apply percentages to her work?*

4 *Do you think she's ready to take her test? If so, can you give a rough timescale?*

Equal opportunities and health and safety

Finding out whether learners are being treated fairly and working safely should also be part of your organisation's tracking system, and requires careful discussion. As a matter of course, you should check out equality of opportunity and health and safety issues at every review and – importantly – take action and record what you have done, writing down anything that may give cause for concern. For more on this, and on what information to give the learner on policies and procedures, see page 31.

Here are some examples of things you would need to record and act on. What targets and action points would you want to include when recording the results of these reviews?

1 Dave has been working at Atlanta Chandlers for 12 months. He receives an annual appraisal every April and the format is the same for all employees. After appraisal all employees get a pay rise dependent upon merit and time served. Dave gets on with everyone in the company, about 10 employees, and has already been on a one-day safe lifting course along with three other employees.

Dave has to go to other departments within the chandlery. The salesroom is small and after a sunny weekend or a bank holiday the fenders, ends of rope reels and packets of fender covers are all over the floor. Dave has mentioned it to the sales staff but they have not taken any notice.

2 Nigel works in a large hotel. There are seven floors and the staff accommodation is on the top floor at the back. When you're reviewing, he tells you that the fire alarm has gone off between 5am and 6am several times and this has often occurred when Nigel has been on a late shift and not gone to bed until well after midnight. It has always been a false alarm and Nigel tells you he's fed up with walking down seven flights of stairs and out into the cold then walking back up again 20 minutes later and that now he doesn't bother to leave his room. It would appear that no one at the hotel checks if everyone has evacuated the building although the procedure states that they should.

You would have to discuss with the learner what they might do; in these cases they must report the potential hazard to the company's heath and safety officer immediately. These situations might give the learner the opportunity to gather evidence for a unit of their NVQ: 102.1 Ensure your own actions reduce risks to health and safety. In the first example, Dave decided to identify the relevant organisational policies and record his actions and the outcome in his log book.

Quality assurance

Quality assuring the review process involves:

- gathering data by:
  - observing reviews
  - sampling reviews from a range of reviewers
  - gathering feedback.

- using the resulting data to:
  - compare performance of reviewers
  - decide what needs to change.

Gathering data

1 Observing

Whatever type of review you use you will need to observe reviewers in action at some point. If you are going to observe, both you and the person carrying out the review need to be clear about what you're observing and the standards required.

For example, you might be looking for:

- opportunities for the learner to ask questions
- the use of open questions by the reviewer
- negotiating and agreeing targets with the learner
- use of positive and negative feedback by the reviewer
- appropriate body language
- use of questions to check progress, equality of opportunity and health and safety
- how the review is managed: for example, timings and choice of venue.

2 Sampling

As all reviews are documented, sampling records is an obvious way to ensure quality. A sample of reviews across occupational areas and reviewers can be selected, and compared using the same set of standards or criteria. For example:

- Are there adequate comments about health and safety, equality of opportunity and progress?
- Have workplace supervisors been involved, and if not have arrangements been made to seek their views?
- Are targets appropriate and SMART?
- Is there continuity between reviews?
- Is progress quantified in some meaningful way for the learner?

3 Gathering feedback

You might want to seek the views of the learners, employers and/or trainers concerning the effectiveness of the review process. You may then need to carry out further investigations into areas of concern.

What providers say

Here are some suggestions for data gathering from providers:

'We asked our employers how useful they found the progress review. We were surprised when a largish percentage said "not at all useful". When we investigated, we found that most of them didn't take part in the process and didn't realise they could. We actively involve all our employers now.'

'When we started gathering data for our QA procedures many of our learners told us they didn't see the point of the review process. Over time, though, satisfaction rates have improved. This is partly because they mature in their outlook to learning while they're with us and also because of our induction process – we make a point of introducing learning and reflection right from the start.'

'We use the Red Amber Green (RAG) system at review with learners to agree how their programme is going. This is not used to judge the learner as a "red" learner, rather to ask: Are they making planned progress? This helps us identify when things have not gone well – it could be that a training session wasn't delivered rather than the learner not turning up, for example. Also, we see reviewing as an opportunity to look at progression within the context of the whole apprenticeship. If a learner has not progressed very well since the last review, we plan how to get back on track with them. In this way the review is an opportunity – a way out, if you like.'

Using data

The data collected can be used to:

- compare performance of staff and learners within a particular occupational area
- compare performance of staff and learners across occupational areas
- highlight learners making slow progress, and the need for action
- ensure that reviews are carried out at the specified time
- pinpoint areas where training or learning may not be working effectively.

It's important to involve all staff in QA procedures such as observations, so that people don't feel they are being judged subjectively or negatively. It's also important for everyone to realise how objective data can help both staff and the organisation to identify areas where improvements could be made.

'We found we were falling behind with the number of reviews. In the construction industry sometimes you arrange an appointment with a learner to do a review but when you get to the site you find they've been moved to another site, or the job has finished, so you have to arrange another one. We're looking to change this.'
Reviewer, construction

'Our reviews showed learners were failing to achieve their key skills. When we investigated further we realised we weren't liaising with our subcontractor closely – we needed to be talking to them about individual learners rather than doing a block booking.'
Training manager

Setting quality criteria

You need to set your own quality criteria for reviewing within your organisation, and make sure everyone signs up to them. One way is to involve all reviewers in drawing up the criteria for themselves. Do this by asking them what they think makes a 'good' review or reviewer.

Here's an example of an observation checklist[7] to get you started:

Quality statement	Yes	No
Are the employer and work-based supervisor involved at some stage in the review?	☐	☐
Does the review record achievements since the last review?	☐	☐
Are key skills achievements discussed and recorded?	☐	☐
Are the learners' views sought and recorded?	☐	☐
Is the review conducted in a suitable environment?	☐	☐
How often are learners reviewed?		
Does the frequency of review vary with the needs of the learner, or do they strictly follow the set pattern? Is there flexibility?		
Are future actions agreed?	☐	☐
Is the review signed and dated by the learner, employer and provider?	☐	☐
Do all those involved receive a copy of the review?	☐	☐
Is the date of the next review recorded on the ILP and review sheet?	☐	☐
Are action points from the last review followed up?	☐	☐
Do reviews refer to the ILP?	☐	☐
Do reviews refer to assessor feedback actions?		

It's important not to lose sight of the reasons why quality assurance – and the review process – are important: ultimately you are ensuring that the learner succeeds on their programme of learning. This means continually striving to improve the quality of learning from the learner's point of view; progress reviews are your main source of information. In addition, the process of reviewing itself, if carried out effectively by skilled reviewers who know how to involve learners, will ensure that learners are equipped to reflect on their own progress in the future.

---

7 © Brian Tritton, 2005. Reproduced with permission.